Devil, Don't Touch My Stuff!

Dr. Ed Dufresne

Ed Dufresne Ministries
Temecula, California

Unless otherwise indicated, all scriptural quotations are from the *King James Version* of the Bible.

Devil, Don't Touch My Stuff!
ISBN 0-940763-04-4
Copyright © 1992 by
Ed Dufresne Ministries
P.O. Box 186
Temecula, CA 92593

Some material in this book was
taken from the book *The Lawsuitor*,
copyright © 1980 by Ed Dufresne.

Published by
Ed Dufresne Ministries
P.O. Box 186
Temecula, CA 92593
U.S.A.

Cover design and book production by
DB & Associates Design Group, Inc.
P.O. Box 52756
Tulsa, OK 74152
Editorial Consultant: Phyllis Mackall

Dedication

This book is lovingly dedicated to my son, Stephen, who is the inspiration for this book. Upon unpacking his toys in the hotel on a ministry trip, 5-year-old Stephen carefully placed his toy sheriff's badge on the shelf in front of them. Then he went to my wife, Nancy, and said, "Do you know what that means, Mommy? That means, *don't touch my stuff!*"

This book was written so adult believers could also grasp the vital concept of the authority Jesus gave us over Satan and his kingdom — the authority that allows us to say, *"Devil, don't touch my stuff!"*

Stephan Dufresne

Contents

Chapter 1
Inspired by a Little Child

The inspiration for this book came from my son, Stephen. Like most ministers, I get insights and even sermons from the things my child says and does.

Stephen, my wife, and I drove to Anaheim not long ago, where we were going to participate in a camp meeting. We checked into a hotel near Disneyland. They gave us a very nice two-bedroom suite. One bedroom was for Stephen, and the master bedroom was for Nancy and me.

Stephen's room had its own television set, so Stephen went into his room with the yellow duffel bag he had brought with him. He started unpacking all of his toys, stacking them on the shelves under the TV set.

Like all 5-year-old boys, he has lots of toy trucks — four-wheel drive trucks, high trucks, and low trucks — plus toy guns and so forth. After he finished arranging the toys to his satisfaction on those shelves, he took his sheriff's badge and propped it in front of all his toys.

I wasn't there when he did this, but his mother was. He got her attention, pointed to the badge, and said, "Mommy, you know what that badge means? *That means, don't touch my stuff!*"

Later, Nancy said, "Do you know what Stephen said today?" When she told me about the badge, the hair rose on the back of my head. The Spirit of God came all over me, and the Lord said, "I have given my people a badge of authority, and that's the Name of Jesus. When they wear that badge, knowing the authority they carry, they have a right to say, *'Devil, don't touch my stuff!'*"

Do you know what your "stuff" is? It's your family, your money, your goods, your house, your health, and anything else that belongs to you.

For example, you should tell the devil to take his hands off your unsaved family members and loose them and let them go in the Name of Jesus. But you must *believe* it when you say it. If you don't believe it, it won't do you any good. Little Stephen *believed* that his sheriff's badge had authority behind it.

How many of you get in fear when you're driving and you see flashing red lights go on behind you? The first thing you think is, "Did I break the speed limit?" Why are you in fear? Because you know that the police officer has authority. He has a badge that says so. That badge gives him authority. His state, county, or town will back him up. My little boy identified with a sheriff's badge that represents authority. He put it in front of his toys and said, "That means, *don't touch my stuff!*"

The Name of Jesus Is Your Badge

That phrase went off in my spirit when I heard it. God dealt with me about the fact that Christians need to know and remind themselves about the authority they have in the Name of Jesus of Nazareth. Actually, *the Name of Jesus is your badge!*

When you get up in the morning, you need to put on the whole armor of God. I'd like to suggest that you see yourself putting on that badge of authority along with the rest of your spiritual armor. When you do, say, *"Devil, don't touch my stuff! Don't touch my stuff! Enough is enough!"*

How many of you have had your paycheck eaten up? The minute you got everything paid off, the car or the washing machine broke down. The Bible says, "Resist the devil, and he will flee from you. Draw nigh to God, and he will draw nigh to you" (James 4:7,8).

What's happening is, people are resisting God and drawing nigh (near) to the devil. This is what I mean: You wake up in the morning, feel pain from that old spirit of arthritis, and say, "Oh, my arthritis!" What you're doing is resisting God. You're resisting healing, and you're drawing nigh to that arthritis.

When you *know* you have a badge of spiritual authority, you can get up in the morning and say to that spirit of arthritis, "No! Get out of here in the Name of Jesus!"

Exercise Your Authority

You've got to walk in your authority! But it doesn't just fall on you like ripe apples; you've got to *exercise* your authority.

My son preached a five-hour sermon just by saying, *"Don't touch my stuff!"*

The devil came around and taunted me, "Look, you've been in the ministry for twenty-five years and your whole family isn't even saved."

I said, "My God meets all of my needs according to His riches in glory by Christ Jesus, and my needs aren't all financial needs. The Bible says to believe on the Lord Jesus Christ and you shall be saved, and all your house" (Acts 16:31). I've been standing on that promise, and just recently some of my family members have made Jesus their Lord.

We're just warming up, friends. We're going to blast out of this place, planet Earth, and the time isn't very far away. The Middle East is warming up for the last battle, the battle of Armageddon, when the blood is going to come up to the horses' bridles (Revelation 14:20).

But before that happens, I predict that we're going to see one of the greatest revivals that this world has ever seen. The people of the world are going to know that Jesus is alive and well!

The Authority of the Believer

Although God has given you the authority of the believer, the Bible says that a doubleminded man or, as one translation reads, "a two-spirited man," won't receive anything from God (James 1:6-8). This kind of a person is up one minute and down the next.

He says, "Well, yes, I'm going to get it. No, I'm not. Yes, I am. No, I'm not. Yes, I am." God said that a person with this kind of attitude will never get anything from Him; the devil will make sure of that!

How many of you know you've got the power of attorney to use the Name of Jesus? Do you know what the power of attorney is? Businessmen do.

Suppose a pastor friend tells me, "Ed, I'm going to preach in Europe for two years, and I'm going to sign my church over to you for that length of time." What he means is, he's going to give me the power of attorney to operate the church *just as if he were here.*

I could sign checks in his name. I could draw money out of the bank. I could run the church just as if he were here — but he's not here; he's in Europe.

Where Satan Gets His Power

This is the same thing Jesus did when He left this earth: He stripped Satan of all his power! Satan doesn't have any power. *The only power or authority he's got is what we give him!*

Some people want deeper revelations, but they haven't even mastered the truths of Mark 11:22-24, that you can have what you say. You can locate people by what they say. You can discover if they have faith or if they're in unbelief.

When you tell the devil, *"Devil, don't touch my stuff,"* say it with authority! In the spirit realm, we believers have authority.

When I get on an airplane, I have authority to believe for a safe flight. Once on board, I take authority over that aircraft and its crew in the Name of Jesus. It doesn't matter if the pilots are drunk or sober. I've got angels to protect me, regardless of the circumstances.

You may say, "You're being egotistical." No, I'm not. We've got to know the difference between being arrogant and knowing *who we are* in Christ.

Never Show Fear

A famous investor who had hit hard times was quoted in a national newspaper as saying, "When an adversary can see fear in your eyes or hear it in your voice, you're as good as dead." When it looked like his empire was falling apart, he said he stayed firm. He didn't show any fear in his eyes or in his voice; he just kept on going. Even though this man is ungodly, he knows something we Christians should adopt.

Who is our adversary? The devil. How much stronger should we be able to stand against our adversary, using the authority we have in the Name of Jesus, than that ungodly man can stand against his adversaries.

The Spirit of Wisdom and Revelation

Now let's look at a passage from Ephesians 1 that will really bless you when you study it:

[I] Cease not to give thanks for you, making mention of you in my prayers,

That the God of our Lord Jesus Christ, the Father of glory, may give unto you the spirit of wisdom and revelation in the knowledge of him:

The eyes of your understanding being enlightened....

Ephesians 1:16-18

I'm not going to confess that I don't know something. I'm going to say instead that I might not have the answer right now, but I'm going to get the answer, because I have the wisdom of God flowing out to me. I have the mind of Christ!

Jesus wasn't stupid, and He didn't promise us the spirit of stupidity. He has given you "...the spirit of wisdom and revelation in the knowledge of him" (verse 18). We need to have the knowledge of Jesus.

What did Jesus really accomplish at Calvary? That's what Paul talks about in First Corinthians 11, when he discusses discerning the Lord's Body:

> **For he that eateth and drinketh unworthily, eateth and drinketh damnation to himself, not discerning the Lord's body. For this cause many are weak and sickly among you, and many sleep [die].**

> **1 Corinthians 11:29,30**

You can take that to mean both physical and spiritual death. Why? Because they don't discern what was provided for them at Calvary.

No one is hanging on that cross — because Jesus isn't there. He isn't dead, and He isn't in any tomb. He's seated at the right hand of the Father.

He came and got us out of the mess Adam got us into. He came and stripped Satan of all his power. He gave us the power of attorney. He gave us the spirit of wisdom and revelation in the knowledge of Him.

What Would Jesus Do?

If Jesus were here right now, what would He do? He would heal the sick. He would cast out devils. He would have the wisdom to know how to handle things. If we want Jesus' kind of wisdom and knowledge, we need to study more about Jesus.

But too many people today are lifting up men instead. Why don't you follow Jesus? He's the best example we've got.

Paul continues his teaching in Ephesians 1:18,19:

> **The eyes of your understanding being enlightened; that ye may know what is the hope of his calling, and what the riches of the glory of his inheritance in the saints,**

> **And what is the exceeding greatness of his power to usward who believe....**

How many of you are believers? He's talking about you and me.

We need a revelation of Jesus. We don't need to be overly concerned about everything that's happening in the world. There are going to be *more* earthquakes in the world. There are going to be *more* wars in the world. There is going to be *more* starvation in the world. The Bible says all these things are going to come, and then the end. We're just seeing prophecy come to pass.

But right in the middle of it, we can have the knowledge of Jesus. We can know, we can be in the know, and we can be helping know what's about to happen.

Do You Ring Hell's Alarm?

Does the devil know you're around? When a righteous man wakes up in the morning, an alarm bell goes off in hell. "He's up!" they shriek in fear. "He knows who he is in Christ. He knows he's been made the righteousness of God. (Righteousness means right standing.) We're in trouble! Get the extra forces! We've had it!"

Have you ever noticed that a police officer gets out of his car with authority? I have never seen one slip out of a police car. They strut out. They *know* they've got authority.

You and I ought to know that we're in right standing with the Father. Every one of us should have a beacon light on the top of our head, like that flashing light that's on top of the police car. It proclaims to the devil and his demons, "I know who I am in Christ Jesus, and I know my authority, buddy."

...and what the riches of the glory of his inheritance in the saints,

And what is the exceeding greatness of his power....

Ephesians 1:18,19

Let's look at that phrase "inheritance in the saints." I recently heard about a family that was about to be cheated out of their inheritance, and the unfairness of it made me very angry and upset.

7

Then God said to me, "Why don't you get that indignant when the devil comes and tells you that he's going to destroy you?"

I replied, "You're right."

Walk in Your Inheritance

We have a right to our heavenly inheritance. Jesus is our Big Brother, and what Jesus got, you and I get. We have a right to it. We didn't make that decision; He did. But we're the ones who must make the decision to *walk in it*.

Do you remember when some devils crossed the line and Jesus locked them up before their time? Devils shouldn't cross the boundary of our authority. If they do, it's because they've talked us out of it.

Have you ever had anyone try to talk you out of your authority? Just try to talk a policeman out of arresting you!

"You have no right to put those cuffs on me."

He responds, "Oh, yeah? Get in the car."

Arrest the Devil!

My son is into toy handcuffs right now. I'll be lying on the couch and he'll come and handcuff me with little plastic cuffs. He'll say, "You're under arrest." That's what you and I ought to do with the devil — *arrest him with the Word of God when he attacks us!* Arrest him when he tries to kill us with sickness! Arrest him when your children become rebellious!

Go in your prayer closet and take authority over that spirit of rebellion. Don't tell the devil, "Now, honey, don't do that." Tell him, "No, in the Name of Jesus! *Devil, don't touch my stuff!*"

Notice what else Paul said in this passage:

...according to the working of his mighty power,

Which he wrought in Christ, when he raised him from the dead, and set him at his own right hand in the heavenly places,

Far above all principality, and power, and might, and dominion, and every name that is named, not only in this world, but also in that which is to come:

And hath put all things under his feet....

Ephesians 1:19-22

Under Our Feet

Wouldn't it be a weird sight if your feet were sticking out of your head, and you were walking around with your shoes up there? But that's the way some Christians view the power of the Church.

They say, "Oh, Jesus has all the power, and He's in heaven, and He's the head of the Church." But Paul said all things were put under our feet. What do the feet belong to? They belong to the Body of Christ, so all things were put under our feet.

It's easy to come to church, sing a chorus about having the devil under our feet, and march around saying, "You're under our feet, Satan." But when you walk out the church doors and sickness tries to come on you, you sing a different tune. Then you say, "O God, help! Do something!"

No, *you* should do something. God has already done everything He's going to do about it. He said for you to take authority over these attacks. He said, "Whatsoever *you* bind on earth shall be bound in heaven" (Matthew 16:19). In other words, God will back up what we say. In fact, it's already backed up, because God has already done it.

In verse 21 we saw the phrase "far above." *Far above!* That's why I'm not frightened of sickness or paralysis anymore. When sickness comes, many people say, "Well, Lord, if You don't heal me, it's going to make me look bad." That's what they're really saying.

Don't worry about your reputation! *In that Name that is far above every name that is named, take authority over that sickness.*

Everything on this earth has a name. There is coming a day when every name on this earth is going to bow their knee

9

to that Name (Hebrews 14:11). Even the ones who curse now, the ones who laugh at you now, and the ones who don't get right with God before they die — they're all going to bow to that Name.

Satan has already been whipped, and he will have to bow to that Name. As a matter of fact, *when you use that Name, Satan can't tell who is using it!* All he can tell is, it's Jesus, because you have the power of attorney to use that Name.

Take Authority Over Lack

Even "lack" is a name. When finances seem like they're coming to a standstill, it's sometimes because we got lackadaisical and didn't take authority over lack.

In our ministry we take authority over lack in the Name of Jesus, and we speak to ministering angels and release them to cause the money to come. Then we pray for our partners' needs to be met by the power of God.

We tithe personally, and our ministry tithes. We're givers. We're always looking for places to plant money, because we know that if we plant, we're going to get a harvest.

My father-in-law, who is a farmer, once said to me, "I've watched you and Nancy. You give airplanes away. You give cars away. You do this and you do that. And I just don't understand it."

God showed me how to answer his question. I said, "Well, why do you go out and dig the dirt up and put seed in?"

He answered, "I do it to make a living."

I said, "That's the reason we do it."

People come to me and complain, "We don't have any money, Brother Dufresne."

I ask them, "Have you planted anything?"

Chapter 2
How To Use the Name of Jesus

Every soldier of the cross should know how to use the Name of Jesus. Actually, it's a weapon. Let's go over to Acts 3 and see what happened to Peter and John one day as they approached the Temple.

> Now Peter and John went up together into the temple at the hour of prayer, being the ninth hour.
>
> And a certain man lame from his mother's womb was carried, whom they laid daily at the gate of the temple which is called Beautiful, to ask alms of them that entered into the temple;
>
> Who seeing Peter and John about to go into the temple asked an alms.
>
> Acts 3:1-3

The first miracle in this account is the fact that two preachers did something together!

Some of you may complain, "Brother Ed, we've heard this story before." You need to hear it again and again until you get it. Faith comes by hearing, and you don't get it by hearing it once; you get faith by hearing it over and over and over again. In fact, most of the Body doesn't understand faith yet.

It's as simple as Stephen with his sheriff's badge. Of course there's no authority in the piece of tin that a sheriff's badge is made out of, but it *represents* the authority that is behind it. Stephen looked at his badge and said, "That means, *don't touch my stuff*." It should be that simple for you

11

and me. Our badge is the Name of Jesus — the authority He gave us.

Dealing With the Devil

Are you fed up with lack? Are you fed up with sickness? Are you fed up with the devil stealing from you? Then do something about it. Say, "Devil, take your hands off my stuff, in the Name of Jesus! *Devil, don't touch my stuff!*" Tell him your "stuff" is off limits, in the Name of Jesus.

Look what happened to Adam: He allowed that snake to get into his garden when he should have taken authority over it. Then he tried to blame his problems on the woman, yet Adam's the one who should have done something about the problem.

Peter did something about the lame man's problem: He exercised his authority over the situation! Notice the authority he used: "And Peter, fastening his eyes upon him with John..." (verse 4).

Expecting To Receive

Peter locked in. He fastened his eyes on the lame man. As you read the account, the lame man said he expected to receive. *If you can get people into expecting to receive, something will happen!*

This is what Nancy does with her tent ministry: She gets the people into an attitude of expectancy.

Nancy advertises free toys, free food, and free clothes, and tells people to come on a certain date to pick it up. But the ticket that entitles them to the free gifts says they've got to come inside the tent first to hear the preaching. For half an hour Nancy gives them a simple Bible lesson on salvation.

They come expecting to get something, and this puts them into an expectant frame of mind. They do receive something in addition to the items: They receive Jesus!

That's what happened to the lame man: He was getting ready to receive, and Peter fastened his eyes on him. When you know who you are in Christ, you're not afraid of sickness or disease. You know who you are — a righteous person. A righteous man is a man who has been made to be in right standing with God. It's just like he never sinned.

Resisting the Devil

How many of you know what the blood of Jesus did for you? Then get off your own case. Some of you beat yourselves up. Some of you look in the mirror, and a voice comes to you — it's the devil — and says, "You're ugly. You're never going to make it. You're too thin. You're too fat. You're bald."

You ought to remind the devil about his past and tell him about his future! The Bible says to resist him and he'll flee from you. It's time for the Body of Christ to rise up and resist him in the Name of Jesus, refusing to accept his lies anymore.

"Brother Dufresne, I'm so far in debt, I'll never get out."

No, just say, "My God meets all of my needs according to His riches in glory, and I'm coming out of debt in the Name of Jesus."

But you say, "It doesn't look like it."

I said, make this confession: "I'm coming out of it."

How the Devil Tricks You

The devil beats more Christians with sin-consciousness than anything else. "You don't have any power," he accuses you after he steals it from you. Resist him! Tell him, *"Devil, don't touch my stuff!"*

Don't forget, I got this concept from a 5-year-old boy, so there's hope for us adults. God used a donkey once to speak to Balaam (Numbers 22), and a minister friend of mine tells a story about a rooster that was used to warn a preacher.

My friend's grandfather was a preacher in the early days of Pentecost. Back then, if you even talked about tongues in some towns, they'd come after you to tar and feather you, beat you up, and leave you out to die!

A mob was coming to tar and feather this man one day. He was sitting on the back porch of a house, and a rooster came up on the porch and started talking to him in English. It said, "They're coming in the front door. Run!" That's right, the Holy Spirit came upon that rooster.

Think about it: If the Lord can use a rooster to prophesy, no telling what we could do if we'd just yield ourselves to God!

We need to get rid of our sense of sin-consciousness. And we need to quit living in the past. Too many Christians mumble, "Well, I'm just an old dirty sinner."

Looking at Us Through the Blood

But the blood of Jesus washed and cleansed us! That's the theme of the Gospel. Put yourself in remembrance of the blood covenant and what God cut for you and me. *The Father looks at us through the blood of His Son!*

It finally dawned on me during the last few years that I'll never be perfect. I've got flaws. I won't be perfect until I see Jesus.

I'm not teaching about being arrogant; I'm teaching about humbling yourself under the mighty hand of God so He can exalt you in due time.

If we could just get that knowledge of how our police officers and others in authority walk in their authority! What would happen to a police officer if he hesitated in the middle of a gun battle? He would die. But that's the same thing Christians are doing every day! They hesitate. They say, "I'm just a dirty old sinner." Then the devil brings up what you did, and you say, "I talked bad last week, or I looked at someone the wrong way, or I shouldn't have been in that place."

Are you going to believe the devil, or are you going to believe your Lord who is in heaven? He said that every name that is named has to bow to that Name. He said, "Ask anything in my name, and I'll give it to you." Hallelujah!

Wake Up to The Final Hour

Quit being drunk on religion and wake up to this hour! These are the last days. There are wars and rumors of war in the natural realm. But there's a war going on in the spiritual realm, and we're right on the threshold of blasting out of this world. We're coming up to the final events.

The wealth of the sinner is laid up for the just. Every time billions of dollars' worth of gold is discovered, rejoice, because it's coming into the kingdom of God. The Bible says so: "The wealth of the sinner is laid up for the just" (Proverbs 13;22).

"That doesn't mean *money*, Brother Dufresne."

Let me lay hands on your head and pray for you. I'm expecting it. It makes me mad when the sinners and the devil-possessed people have all the good things in life and you go to church and see Christians who are just barely making it.

They pull up to church in an old, broken-down car when there's a bunch of sinners out there with brand-new cars. Those blessings are laid up for us, too. We need to take authority over our circumstances and demand for those blessings to come into the kingdom of God in the Name of Jesus. Demand their release from Satan's hand.

Protecting Your Children

The devil is stealing our kids. People take their kids to church and tell them, "God heals." But nothing ever happens in that church. The children never see any miracles. They've been in that church all their life, and when they get older, they ask, "What are you talking about? I've never seen anyone healed!"

Then a young mother dies of a disease. It's no put-down — praise God she's in heaven — but she died too young. The preacher says, "The Lord giveth and the Lord taketh away." And the mother's little child says, "Why should I serve God? He killed my mother."

Come on — we're living in a real world. Those kids know more than you think they know. You don't need to apologize for God. Walk and believe what God says, and then your kids will believe it. You won't have to tell them, "Well, it works sometimes." They'll know it works all the time.

I was away holding a meeting and Nancy called to say, "Stephen is sick. He's doubled over in pain."

I said, "Get him on the phone."

I prayed for him. I said, "Satan, in the Name of Jesus, take your hands off Stephen."

The next day she called again. I asked, "How's Stephen?"

She said, "What did you tell him?"

I said, "I told the devil to take his hands off him."

She said, "When you prayed for him on the phone, the pain left, but after you hung up the phone, the pain came back. We went into the den so he could lie on the couch. I went into the kitchen to get him something to drink. When I came back into the room, I heard him say, "I command you to go. I command you to go." Then all of a sudden he shouted, "It's all gone! It's all gone!"

Instill Godly Principles

This is a 5 year old. This is the time in his life to put those principles in him and let him see it work.

Right now in my spirit I see an army of young people rising up. These are young people who aren't going to back down. They're going to believe what the Bible says.

That's what I like about the home schooling program. People are bringing their children up around the Word of God. They aren't around rebellion all day in a secular school.

The reason most kids are the way they are is because the parents don't want to take the time to discipline them and put the Word of God in them. The parents are "too busy" doing things like watching television, going bowling, and so forth. "We don't have time," they say. So they let some ungodly teenager babysit, and they all sit around watching dirty movies!

And you wonder why people have problems with their children? It's time to walk righteously before God! It's time to live it! God gave us authority, and it's time we picked it up and used it.

Most prisons are filled with convicts who were abused either sexually or mentally when they were innocent little children. They didn't get the love they needed from drunken fathers who slapped them around. It isn't entirely their fault, yet we must deal with the problems they created by breaking the law.

Look on Us!

So here was this lame man begging by the side of the road. No telling how many times he was there when Jesus walked into the Temple, but nothing happened then. But Peter fastened his eyes on the man and said, "Look on us!"

The statement "Look on us!" sounds very egotistical to the natural, religious mind. What do you mean, "Look on us"? But Peter didn't say it in an egotistical manner. He said, "Look on us — we've got authority. We can help you."

We, too, need to be bold — not arrogant — and walk in that type of authority.

Praise God for special meetings, but you don't need to have a healing evangelist come to town to get people healed. The Bible says, "Lay hands on the sick and they shall recover." Isn't that what Jesus said in the Great Commission? Do you realize that Jesus was giving us the authority to go and heal the sick?

The lame man paid attention to Peter and John: "And he gave heed unto them, expecting to receive something of them. And Peter said, "Silver and gold have I none; but such as I have give I thee..." (verses 5 and 6).

Peter didn't have any money just then, but not everyone needs money. There are people who would give all their wealth to be happy.

What did Peter have? "Such as I have I give thee: In the name of Jesus Christ of Nazareth rise up and walk." *That Name! Peter had that Name!*

What is invested in that Name? Just what happened at the healing at the Gate Beautiful? Peter and John were identified with Jesus' character and His purpose. They had His delegated power and authority.

If a friend gave me the power of attorney to use his name, I need to identify with the power I got in his name.

Put on Your Badge

There are people who are yelling at God, "God, do something about the devil!" when He's already given *you* the authority to do something. You've got the badge; you just won't put it on. You've put it in a glass case. You're using it as a shrine; you're worshipping it!

Consider what the policeman does when he leaves his house. Doesn't he put his badge on as he walks out the door when he's on duty? That gives him the authority to walk as an officer. Have you seen movies where a policeman flashes his badge at people to prove his authority? That's what I do to the devil in the Name of Jesus!

Enough was enough, in Peter's eyes. We should repeat that phrase to ourselves over the problem we are facing: *"Enough is enough!"*

Healing came into the lame man's ankles because Peter walked in his rightful authority.

We should take our authority over the devil!

Chapter 3
How To Fight the Good Fight of Faith

I'm mad at sickness and disease! I'm mad at the devil for robbing people when he doesn't have any power! Do you know the devil is a deceiver?

Either Jesus paid for our healing on the cross, or He didn't. He did it, as far as I'm concerned. It's settled in my heart and mind. As a matter of fact, when I got it settled in my heart that God still heals people today, that God sets people free, and that it's His will for people to be healed, healthy, and prosperous, it got me kicked out of my *Full Gospel* church!

I also found out it was God's will for me to have power in my life. I didn't have to be a little weakling who whimpered. Yet some say, "You just never know what God might do." But I know what God will do: He'll do what He says in His word. I refuse to let the devil steal my family, kill my kids, or rob from me.

A Diet That Will Kill You

Religion will teach you how to be sick. This error has even crept into Charismatic churches. It is a deceptive lie. Did you know that the church you go to could be a matter of life or death for you! You need to go to a church where they preach the Bible and victory, not a diet of unbelief.

I want you to look at a scripture from First Corinthians 11. I preach a lot out of First Corinthians; especially from the twelfth through the fourteenth chapters. This is from First Corinthians 11, beginning with verse 23:

For I have received of the Lord that which also I delivered unto you, That the Lord Jesus the same night in which he was betrayed took bread:

And when he had given thanks, he brake it, and said, Take, eat: this is my body, which is broken for you: this do in remembrance of me.

After the same manner also he took the cup, when he had supped, saying, This cup is the new testament in my blood: this do ye, as oft as ye drink it, in remembrance of me.

1 Corinthians 11:23-25

"Remembrance" means to remind or call to mind and believe it. The phrase "in remembrance of me" doesn't mean "in memory of." Many people take Communion in memory of "poor Jesus." Don't say "poor Jesus," because He's seated on the right hand of the Father, and He's already passed His test!

What Jesus is saying is that we are to renew our minds and put ourselves into remembrance of what was provided for us on Calvary. One of the things Jesus has provided is that He stripped Satan of all his power and authority!

The Source of Satan's Power

"If this is so," you may ask, "where does Satan get his power today?" He gets it from you and me!

Satan is a leech. The Bible says he goes around as a roaring lion. He *isn't* a lion; he goes around *as* a roaring lion. In other words, he goes around *imitating* a lion — and his roar can be very loud.

Doctors may have diagnosed cancer in your body — and you shake with fear.

After two women got healed of cancer in a healing service in the early '50s, the devil returned to them and tried to put symptoms back on them. One of the women resisted his tricks in the Name of Jesus. But the other said, "Well, I guess I didn't get my healing," and she died.

When an autopsy was performed, they couldn't find one trace of cancer in her body. The devil killed her with *symptoms!* That's how he defeats most of us. Put yourself in remembrance of what Jesus did for us.

We're not to go back, remember what men did to Jesus, and cry over "poor Jesus."

What the Lord is saying is, "Put yourself into remembrance of what I provided for you at Calvary. Put yourself into remembrance that I've given you power and deliverance in my Name. Walk in it, and don't forget it." That's what "put into remembrance" means: Don't forget what manner of man or woman you are.

There's Authority in the Name of Jesus

Now let's look at Luke 10:17. Most of you are familiar with it. If you're not, you soon will be.

And the seventy returned again with joy, saying, Lord, even the devils are subject unto us through thy name.

Through thy name, through thy name, through that Name! The seventy reported, "Lord, even the devils are subject unto us *through that Name!*" Just as my little son knew his sheriff's badge had authority, the seventy learned that Jesus' Name has authority.

And he said unto them, I beheld Satan as lightning fall from heaven.

Behold, I give unto you power to tread on serpents and scorpions, and over all the power of the enemy: and nothing shall by any means hurt you.

Luke 10:18,19

What does "all" mean? Everything. All power, the whole thing — everything. "And nothing shall by any means hurt you." You can read Psalm 91 if you want to study everything Jesus is talking about here.

All the power of the enemy — Jesus put it all under our feet! The feet belong to the Body of Christ, so these things are under *our* feet.

When you go around talking about your lack of money all the time, that's what you're going to have: lack. Talk instead about the goodness of God. Repeat scriptures like, "My God shall supply all your need according to his riches in glory by Christ Jesus" (Philippians 4:19).

Stay Hot for God

Do you know the Bible says that the devil is the father of *flies?* That's right; his name was Beelzebub. He's the father of flies! Have you ever seen flies land on a hot stove? No, they land on cold ones. If you stay hot for God, the devil and his forces won't be able to defeat you.

If you stay hot for God, you won't be going around complaining, "The devil did this and the devil did that to me." He isn't going to steal from you when you're hot for God! That's what happened to Timothy. Paul told him, "Stir up the fire that's within you. Keep that stirred up." We need to stay in the Word of God and renew our minds with it.

During the last three years, I've been seeing in the natural that *the healing anointing has been turned up.* This is the hour to take back what belongs to us!

I've heard that a panther has such a menacing scream that deer standing around a water hole will freeze with fear when they hear it. Then the panthers can go and pick their prey. This is how the devil uses fear against us — even though all things have been put under our feet.

Fight Fear With Faith

We need to walk in that great truth and take authority over the devil. I know we've heard this before, but we haven't heard it enough. We need to hear it over and over again. Pastors need to preach it over and over and over again, for "Faith cometh by hearing, and hearing by the Word of God."

This isn't the hour to back off from fear of Satan — this is the hour to go forward!

In Chapter 1, we looked at Ephesians 1:18,19:

The eyes of your understanding being enlightened; that ye may know what is the hope of his calling, and what the riches of the glory of his inheritance in the saints,

And what is the exceeding greatness of his power to usward who believe....

Let's pick up there and continue the thought:

...according to the working of his mighty power,

Which he wrought in Christ, when he raised him from the dead, and set him at his own right hand in the heavenly places,

Far above all principality, and power, and might, and dominion, and every name that is named, not only in this world, but also in that which is to come:

And hath put all things under his feet....

Ephesians 1:18-22

His power is for us to use against the devil, because we understand what Jesus did for us. We understand that we have authority over the devil. We understand that we have power in the Name of Jesus.

Catch a Case of Healing

"Brother Dufresne, I don't like my circumstances."

Well, change your circumstances! Quit bragging on the devil. Instead of complaining when you sneeze with cold symptoms, "Oh, the devil's putting something on me," just declare, "I'm catching healing for sure, glory to God!" And that's what you'll get!

That's what I do. If someone asks, "Are you coming down with a cold," I reply, "No, I'm coming up with healing."

"Oh, you're one of those confession guys."

Yes, I'm made in the image of God. I'm seated with Christ, far above all principality, and power, and might, and dominion, and every name that is named. So sickness and disease are under my feet.

Let's go over to Hebrews 10:

Cast not away therefore your confidence [your boldness], which hath great recompence of reward.

For you have need of patience, that, after ye have done the will of God, ye might receive the promise.

For yet a little while, and he that shall come will come, and will not tarry.

Now the just shall live by faith....

Hebrews 10:35-38

The Just Live by Faith

If you aren't living by faith, you aren't living! The just live by *faith*.

When the Lord told me to move to California from Tulsa, I got into unbelief over my church building. We put it on the market, and several people wanted it, yet God kept dealing with me not to use the building for a secular purpose, such as manufacturing. Even though it was a metal building, it was finished beautifully inside.

I really got into unbelief about that building. In fact, I got doubleminded about it. When I saw that, I changed my unbelief into faith.

One day I was in an airplane, and God spoke to me. He said, "Your test is over with. You have been proven." That blessed me! The devil will come and test you, but God will prove you.

He said, "You're to go to California, and you'll be richly blessed." He said some more, and concluded, "That's my will."

Then He asked me a question. When God asks you a question, you'd better listen to what He's saying.

He said, "What would you do if you already had a buyer for your building?"

"Well, I'd start packing."

He didn't say any more.

24

Finally I understood. "That's it! That's it!" I said. I phoned my office. I said, "Start packing!"

"Oh, you got a contract on the building," my staff said.

"No, not in the natural — but *by faith* it's sold. God said it was sold."

So we started packing. And when the last box was almost packed, the deal came through for another ministry to buy our building.

But I wrestled with the sale of that building for a whole year. My wife told me, "You're in unbelief over that building." I said, "No, I'm not!" I got mad! I said, "You're just being a bossy woman." You preachers know that when your wife is in faith and you're in unbelief, you don't want to admit it. Let's just be honest about it. It's all right to be honest.

She was right: I was being doubleminded. We can slip into unbelief so quickly. One minute we can be talking faith, and before you know it, things happen and unbelief gets on us.

God says in His Word, "Now the just shall live by faith: but if any man draw back, my soul shall have no pleasure in him" (Hebrews 10:38). This isn't the hour to draw back! This is the hour to go *forward*, not backwards.

Faith Has No Reverse Gear

Brother Lester Sumrall doesn't even like to ride in a car that's put in reverse gear! He screams, "*Stop!* I don't go backwards! Go around the block if you missed your turn." He explains, "If you go backwards, the devil's got you." (You might think that's rather strange, but at least he's making his point.)

"But the just shall live by faith: but if any man draw back...." I was drawing back; I was almost demanding with my unbelief that God sell that building. My attitude was, "I'm not moving until that building is sold, bless God." I really thought I was in faith, but I wasn't. God told me I wasn't. I was in unbelief!

We often don't live by faith. For example, we dwell on the circumstances that hinder us: We don't have enough money. We can't get where we want to go. We don't realize that we're talking unbelief.

Where did you get those thoughts? "I guess the devil gave them to me." If they aren't in line with the Word of God, I'd reject them, if I were you.

How To Fight Satan, Spiritually

I was in a meeting once, and the church members were really getting with it! The whole place was full of enthusiastic prayer warriors. I liked their zeal! I'd rather have a little wildfire than no fire at all; I'd rather have a little excess than have a mortuary.

I walked up to one brother who was jumping all over and punching the air. As the Spirit leads, I jump all over and dance in the Spirit, but I wanted to find out what the punching was all about.

I asked, "What are you doing?"

He said, "I'm fighting the devil!"

I said, "You are? Can I ask you something? You'd really be getting him good, *if* he had some flesh — but he's a spirit. He has no flesh and blood. How are you going to hurt the devil by punching the air like that? You can't. If you could, just put your boxing gloves out and whip him real good. But you can't fight him that way; you've got to resist him with the Word of God!"

I wasn't trying to hurt the man's feelings — in fact, the microphone was turned off, and no one heard our conversation — but I believe our actions need to be in line with the Bible.

Don't get upset. We need to learn. We can go to extremes on each end. I've been in what you call Charismatic churches, and there was no life in them at all. On the other hand, you can have just the letter of the Word and kill everyone (2 Corinthians 3:6)!

This is the best interpretation of spiritual warfare, and it's simple: God says we're to fight the good fight of faith — and the way we beat the devil is *with the Word of God.* We also fight him with our good confession, because the just shall live *by faith*, and he can't handle that.

This doesn't take away from intercession, and it doesn't take away from people who truly go into the Spirit. Just because some have gotten off in the area of intercession doesn't mean the whole Church should stop praying!

Say No to the Devil!

The important thing is to stay lined up with the Word of God in whatever you do. The devil doesn't want you to do that. He doesn't want you to find out about the authority you have as a result of Jesus' sacrifice on the cross.

Satan has been stripped of all his power. If you have symptoms of sickness, if it tries to latch itself onto you, or even if the doctor says you're sick, you just say, *"No,* in the Name of Jesus! By His stripes I'm healed!"

The way you fight the good fight of faith and run the devil off is with the Word of God. Learn to say no to the devil! Do you know how to say no?

This reminds me of the story of Smith Wigglesworth, who was watching a woman and her little dog one day at a bus stop. The little dog had followed her to the bus stop, and was standing there wagging its tail.

She tried to get it to go home. She said kindly, "Go on, go on home, dear. Get out of here." But the dog wouldn't leave. It just kept wagging its tail. She said, "Go on, now. Get out of here. Go home." Still the dog refused to obey.

Finally she stomped her foot and yelled, "I said — *get out of here!"* And the dog ran home.

Smith Wigglesworth shouted out, "That's how you've got to treat the devil!"

Some of us handle cancer the way that woman handled her little dog. We say weakly, "Oh, cancer, now get away. I'm God's property...I wonder if God's putting this on me to teach me something..."

I'm not trying to make fun of anyone; this is the truth. We Christians are letting victories slip by us. We need to get back on the Word of God, back on faith, and back on healing. There's a whole new generation coming up that's never heard these truths!

Wear Your Badge of Authority

You *have* authority, and you need to be as sure of it as my son is of his toy sheriff's badge. His confession about his badge was revelation knowledge to me. You should wear your badge, too; your badge of authority in that Name. *There's power in that Name of Jesus, glory be to God!*

The way to destroy the devil is by fighting the good fight of faith. And the way to get back everything the devil has stolen from you is to make a stand and declare, "Enough is enough, devil! I want my peace, my joy, my possessions, and everything else that you've stolen from me!"

Before I was saved, I was hardly ever sick, except for having hangovers when I was drinking. That's before I was a Christian. When I got in the Full Gospel church, they taught me how to be sick and to suffer for Jesus.

"Well, we've got to suffer."

"How are you doing?"

"Going through the valley. I just know that some way or another, God's trying to teach me something."

Know Your Enemy

You've got to realize that it's the devil who steals, kills, and destroys. He's the enemy you've got to deal with. It's not your brother-in-law, it's not your son-in-law, and it's not your mother-in-law you're fighting.

You're not fighting against flesh and blood! You can't beat on the devil with your fists. This is a *spiritual* fight that you can only win with the Word of God!

You can war all night, beat yourself, get all sweaty, and everything else. The devil will just sit there and laugh at you. If you want to dance around, I'm all for it, but use the Word of God with it.

I don't want to dampen your fire or enthusiasm; I want you to have victory when you fight the devil. Stay aligned with the Word of God. Don't be like some, who are getting so far out, they're getting into error.

Look at James 1:5. It says:

If any of you lack wisdom, let him ask of God, that giveth to all men liberally, and upbraideth not; and it shall be given him.

Confess, "I'm not a dodo anymore. I've got the wisdom of God." Say it again. You need to say it until you start believing it. You need to hear your own voice say it. The more you say it, the more you believe it.

Don't Waver in Faith

The next verses continue the thought:

But let him ask in faith, nothing wavering. For he that wavereth is like a wave of the sea driven with the wind and tossed.

For let not that man think that he shall receive any thing of the Lord.

James 1:6,7

This passage answers a lot of questions. We want to blame our problems on everyone and everything else, but they land right back on our own doorstep.

For example, I knew a tremendous man of God who died recently. He was in his 50's. He pastored a large church. He was always there for his flock. They could call him at 3 o'clock in the morning and he would counsel and pray with them.

But this brother was grossly overweight. And he wouldn't rest his body. God dealt with him about losing the weight, but he wouldn't do it. You can't break natural laws and have your body last forever. There are things you are responsible for in the natural realm.

My wife says it this way: The greater the anointing, the smaller the margin for error. In other words, baby Christians can make all kinds of mistakes and get away with it, but more mature Christians are accountable for what they know.

We've heard of ministers falling over dead right and left. Why? Because once they know to do certain things, not to do them is sin.

The Pastor Who Lacked Wisdom

Why did that wonderful pastor die when he was only 50-some years old? I'll tell you what happened: He got robbed! Yes, he's in heaven, but he left a family with young children and a church of 3,500 people who loved him dearly. Of course, he's going to get rewards for what he did on earth. But let's face it: he, his family, and his congregation got robbed of many fruitful years of his life and ministry.

Because he didn't listen to the Holy Spirit, this pastor burned the midnight oil and burned his body up. We've got to be obedient to the Word. We can't live the way we want to, burning the midnight oil and never resting. These bodies of ours aren't supernatural. They're still flesh and blood!

God never told us to burn out.

Running on Empty

Do you know why we ministers burn out? It's because we do things that God never gave us the oil to do, and we burn our bearings out trying to be a jack-of-all-trades.

I'm just getting started. I've been in the ministry 25 years now, and I want you to know I'm just getting started. Quit talking about your past. Quit talking about your gray hair. Quit talking about your arthritis. The reason it's *yours* is because you talk about it all the time!

Be like Smith Wigglesworth. Get up in the morning and say, "I don't ask my body how it feels; I tell it!"

I feel like I'm 15 years old! Maybe you got started late in the things of God, like I did, but you aren't late when it comes to the Word of God. You can get up in the morning and God will give you the strength to do a dance in the Spirit that some 15 year old couldn't do. We believers shouldn't be *retiring;* we should be *refiring!*

Some say, "I need rest," but they don't even know what they need rest from, because they haven't *done* anything!

Grace To Travel

Men have said, "I want to travel with you" — until they do. They last four days. We're in and out of airports, preaching every night, going here, going there, doing this, doing that. You've got to be *anointed* to withstand that kind of a schedule! You've got to know the Word of God.

After several days of this whirlwind, they say, "We don't know how you do it!" I tell them, "It's the grace of God."

I've had pastors accompany me on trips, but after three days they're homesick. They're on the phone to their wives half the time, wailing, "Oh, darling, I miss you so much!"

I can travel like this because God gave me the grace for what I'm doing. If pastors did it, they'd get burned out, because they don't have the anointing to do it. But if I tried to stay home and pastor, I'd be climbing the walls.

Someone offered me a church not too long ago. He said, "The people love you."

I said, "They don't need me. They need a pastor. I'd leave them."

"What do you mean?"

"After two or three weeks, I'd be climbing the walls. I'd be grouchy. I'd be growling at everyone!"

Why? Because I'm supposed to be out on the road. That's my job.

The Loser: A Doubleminded Man

Notice what the Bible said in James 1:7,8: "For let not that man think that he shall receive any thing of the Lord. A double minded man is unstable in all his ways." This means an undecided or two-spirited person. One minute they say they've got it, and the next minute they say they don't have it. A doubleminded person won't get what he wants. That's what the Bible says. So we must be singleminded about the Word of God.

I was on a boat the other day. I seldom fish, but I did go deep sea fishing. We were looking for seaweed, because the fish are usually found under the seaweed.

The way the sea tosses a boat up and down is similar to the ups and downs of people's faith. One minute they're *up* — their faith is high — and the next minute they're *down* — they've seemingly lost their faith.

That's when they begin to say, "Well, we don't know. We don't understand. We're good Christians, but this thing happened. We pay our tithes. We just don't understand..."

I understand. Go after the devil! You're Christians. The only power He has is what *you* give him. Didn't Jesus tell us that Satan has been stripped of his power? Do you believe Jesus? Isn't that what He said? Jesus has given us *all* power over the devil.

We need to put the badge of our authority on, wear it, believe it, and put ourselves into remembrance that we have the power of attorney to use that Name and tell the devil no.

Say, "No, devil! Take your hands off my finances. Take your hands off my body — now! In the Name of Jesus, I want everything back that you've stolen from me through the years!"

The Devil Makes Them Do It

People who have stolen from you or have lied about you are not your problem. Flesh and blood is not your problem; it's the devil who leads them to do those things as they yield to him.

For example, when a man commits adultery, that act didn't start that very day. He didn't think just out of the blue, "I think I'll go out and get another woman today." No, the devil worked on that man's thought life for a matter of weeks, months, or even years, and the man accepted the thoughts.

He whispered to him, "Your wife doesn't love you. She doesn't satisfy you. No one cares about you. You poor old guy, you work in the church and no one cares." The man didn't resist these thoughts, and then the devil's deceptions took root, and the end result was sin and destruction.

Chapter 4
Doers of the Word, Not Hearers Only

But be ye doers of the word, and not hearers only, deceiving your own selves.

For if any be a hearer of the word, and not a doer, he is like unto a man beholding his natural face in a glass:

For he beholdeth himself, and goeth his way, and straightway forgetteth what manner of man he was.

James 1:22-24

That's the problem right there: deception.

You're deceiving yourself if you say, "Yes, I love Jesus, but I don't believe in paying my tithes." You aren't hurting the church — God will take care of the church — you're really hurting yourself.

"Well, God doesn't heal today." You're deceiving yourself, and some preacher helped you deceive yourself.

"Well, we just never know if it's God's will or not." The reason people say that is because they're doubleminded.

And why are you worrying about finances when God said He'd meet all your needs according to His riches in glory by Christ Jesus?

"Brother Dufresne, you don't know. I love my house, but I went bankrupt."

Don't you think God can restore that?

"But our life savings are gone."

35

I'm not belittling your plight, but God can breathe out of His left nostril and give it all back to you, if you'll just believe Him.

Plant Your Seed

Plant the seed for whatever it is you lack.

"I don't have any clothes."

Start "planting" clothes, then.

James continues his message:

But whoso looketh into the perfect law of liberty, [the Word of God] **and continueth therein, he being not a forgetful hearer, but a doer of the work, this man shall be blessed in his deed.**

James 1:25

I like that. This man is a doer of the Word of God, and he will be blessed. Whatever the Word says I am, that's who I am. I don't care what I *feel* like.

Sometimes I wake up and I don't even feel saved! How about you? If we went by feelings, we wouldn't feel saved. Sometimes I don't feel prosperous. Ask my bank book. Have you ever looked in your bank book, and it says you're not prosperous?

We lay our ministry bank book down and we break the power of the devil. We're givers. We tithe on everything that comes into our ministry.

We also plant seed, because we believe the scripture that says, "Give, and it shall be given unto you." We tell Satan, "Take your hands off our money!" We release ministering angels to cause the money to come, and it comes.

Working Out Spiritually

A famous leader in the communications industry had to get up recently and apologize for saying that Christians are losers. He said he was reared in a strong Christian home, but one of his family members died, and it seemed to him that their prayers weren't answered. What he was really saying was, "They preached one thing, but we never saw anyone get healed."

I wonder how many children who are in church today who will develop that same attitude later in life. "Yeah, God heals today," they hear their parents say as they're popping pain pills and everything else into their mouth.

I didn't say that taking medicine is a sin but, on the other hand, when you mature and get knowledge of the Word of God, you ought to believe the Word.

Why wait until cancer hits you to believe God for healing? Why don't you start with headaches? Instead of taking an aspirin, why don't you go turn that TV off, get into the Word of God, and run that headache off? That's how to develop your faith for healing. That's how you "work out," spiritually speaking.

Instead of sitting there watching television and videos, you could be studying the Word of God. Don't wait until some tragedy comes and say, "Oh, we don't know why this happened. We're good Christians." You were watching movies and videos all the time, and now you're blaming God because you have no faith for healing!

Destroyed for Lack of Knowledge

For this cause [not discerning what Jesus purchased for them at Calvary] many are weak and sickly among you, and many sleep [die]" (1 Corinthians 11:30). You don't get too popular preaching that at a funeral!

We read this scripture earlier when we discussed the 350-pound pastor whose life ended too early because he didn't discern how to treat his body properly. His wife said he never slept normally; he burned the midnight oil and worked all night. His body couldn't take it. He burned out.

We're destroyed, the Bible tells us, for lack of knowledge. We've got to get back to the Word. *The devil has been defeated, but he uses our lack of knowledge to destroy us.*

Resist the Devil!

Another reason we're defeated is because we won't fight him. We need to do more than just hold our ground; we need to take back what belongs to us!

But he giveth more grace. Wherefore he saith, God resisteth the proud, but giveth grace [or ability] unto the humble.

Submit yourselves therefore to God. Resist the devil, and he will flee from you.

James 4:6,7

Actually "grace" is ability. God will give you the ability to do your job, whatever He has called you to do, and He will give you the ability to stand on the Word. He calls on you to resist the devil. How do you resist him? By saying no!

I've got a little boy who likes toys. And every supermarket or store we go to, I know what he's going to say. "Daddy, can I have a toy?"

He'll work on us. Some children fall on the floor and have fits to get their way, but we don't allow Stephen to have fits. If you let children have fits when they're small, they'll have worse fits when they become teenagers. They'll just do it a different way. So we don't allow him to have fits; we take authority over that.

Nevertheless, he'll try to wear us down to buy toys for him. Children are darlings, but they'll wear you down. They'll stay after it. *The Lord says that's the way the devil is: He'll stay after you!*

Many people let their children run wild. When they're as young as ten years old, they're running the house, all because their parents don't want to be bothered. We can't take that attitude. We must raise our children properly.

Learn To Say No

We also must learn how to say no to them — and to the devil, because the devil will resist you and resist you and

38

resist you until he breaks you down. But the Bible says if you'll resist him, he'll flee from you.

Notice James says, "Resist the devil, and he will flee from you. Draw nigh to God..." (James 4:7,8). Unfortunately, many people draw nigh to the devil and resist God! They resist His Word.

You can tell them, "The Bible says you're healed."

"Well, I know that, but..."

They draw nigh to the symptoms. They draw nigh to what someone else said. They draw nigh to what the medical report said instead of drawing nigh to the Word of God.

There's a devil-hunting fad going on now. They're spitting up into jars and saying that's devils — all kinds of stupid things. They even want to talk to the devils.

Well, that devil will fool you. He'll say, "I was in George Washington," or someone else in the past. These foolish people think they're getting genuine information, but the devils are laughing at them and lying to them.

How To Talk to Devils

I don't want to talk to devils. I tell them, "Get out, in the Name of Jesus! Loose that person and let him go!" I don't want any devil telling me things. (They always lie, anyway.)

Yes, there are devils. They are real. But they are also deceivers. They'll tell a little child, "Your parents don't love you. They don't care about you."

God told me something that flat set me free. He said, "People need to realize there are familiar spirits out there."

What is a familiar spirit? It's a spirit that's familiar with you. There are spirits that come down through families. They know all about your family. They also know how to push your "button" when you're on a high and cause you to drop real low — because they're "familiar" with you. They get around you and put you down.

The Holy Spirit would never put you down. The Holy Spirit would never tell you you're ugly and no good. The

39

Holy Spirit would never say that. Of course, He convicts you of sin, but He never puts you down.

It's those familiar spirits that have been dogging you all your life that put you down. For example, sometimes you get to a certain point in life, like in your marriage, and that devil knows how to push that button to deceive you into getting a divorce. You ought to say, "No, no, in the Name of Jesus, I resist you! No! God says I'm a man of God."

These deceiving familiar spirits will also convince you that people won't accept you because you're the wrong color, the wrong size, or something else. "You're white and you've got green eyes. You're black. You're brown. You're red. You're yellow. You're too big. You're too small. They won't accept you."

This is real life. Those familiar spirits use all those combinations, because they know you. They know your family. They know where to come and push that button to keep you down all the time.

How To Resist Devils

We're supposed to resist them in the Name of Jesus and *say what God says about us:* "I'm a child of the King. He has made me the righteousness of God. Yes, I've got flaws, but I want you to know, devil, that the blood of Jesus covers those flaws! And, glory be to God, when God looks at me through the blood of Jesus, I'm perfect in His eyes!" Resist the devil, and he will flee from you. He'll split!

Every day you wake up, he's trying to resist you. Sometimes it takes an effort to get out of bed, doesn't it? Some mornings I wake up and the devil says, "You've got arthritis." He'll even try to put the symptoms in my joints.

He will say, "You've been going too much. You preached so hard last night, you perspired, and now you've caught pneumonia." He'll even give me a tickle in my throat and cause me to cough.

I get mad and jump out of bed. "How do you like *that*, devil?" I yell. And he goes. That's resisting him.

The Devil's Trying To Rob You

Or the devil will come after you with a lack, usually in finances. The office machine will break down; then your car. You say, "I don't understand why that car keeps breaking down!" I understand it. The devil's trying to rob you; he's trying to steal from you. He does it by using one bill here and another bill there.

You may make good money, but when all of your equipment breaks down, it's a way the devil robs you, because people may charge you too much or rip you off to fix it.

Tell the devil to take his hands off your property! Tell him, "That's enough!"

You've got to stay after those familiar spirits. You've got to fight the good fight of faith — and it is a fight. You've got to make an effort. You can't just lay around and assume, "Whatever will be will be." I'll tell you what will be: The devil will be! So wake up, resist him, and fight!

If you're going to war — if you're going to be a soldier — you've got to put your spiritual equipment on and fight the good fight of faith. That's how you whip the devil. Paul said, "I fight the good fight."

Every day you're going to have to resist.

"Well, I get tired."

Big deal. All of us get tired. It's the devil who wants you to quit fighting, but resist him, in the Name of Jesus.

Deal With Those Familiar Spirits

God is still on His throne, and He has given the believer the authority to do something with the devil. God isn't going to do anything with the devil; He already did what He's going to do.

That's what we must teach people. They need to realize who they are in Christ and quit listening to those familiar spirits telling them, "You're no good. You're this. You're that. You know cancer has been running in your family for many generations, and you're going to die the same way!"

No! Stop it right there. When the devil brings up all those things, resist him. The Holy Spirit would never bring up all that junk. Why? *Because it isn't recorded in heaven.*

Don't Watch the Devil's Home Movies

If you've been washed in the blood of Jesus, your past is not recorded in heaven anymore, so why should you listen to the devil and see all those "pictures" of the past sins that he brings up in your mind.

He'll tell you, "You know how it was with you as a child: You lived in poverty, your dad beat you, and thus and so..." Resist him!

Tell him, "No, I don't want to see that movie, devil. Wait a minute, devil — I'm seeing a *better* movie! I see Jesus up on the cross. I see the blood of Jesus Christ flowing down from that cross. I'm underneath that cross, and His blood is all over me, washing me. And I will not lose my mind. I will not die like my relatives died. I will live until I'm satisfied. Hallelujah, I will finish my course!"

Some people worry, "I think I'm losing my mind!"

Well, that's good. Lose that old thing and get the mind of Christ in there! That squirrely thing just gets mixed up. Someone once joked, "My mind went out to lunch and never did come back." Let the mind of Christ come in and take over.

The devil will have a nervous breakdown if you do that! He'll have to take horse-sized valium.

The Devil's Latest Problem

A group is rising up that he isn't going to be able to keep down like he has some in the past. This group is demanding, "Enough is enough, devil! I'm tired of living in poverty. I'm breaking poverty and every other negative force that's in my family line. Everything I own isn't going to break down any-more to rob me of what belongs to me. In the Name of Jesus Christ of Nazareth, *take your hands off my stuff, devil!"*

It's Too Late To Warn Me

Someone once told me, "God's done away with faith."

I said, "Is that right? You can't sell *me* that bill of goods, because you're too late! I found out that faith works, and I found out that religious stuff doesn't work."

When I was still attending the Full Gospel church, some of the deacons came to visit me in the middle of the night to tell me, "Brother Ed, you're in error with this faith stuff." It broke my heart when they said that.

Years later, one of those deacons phoned me in Florida. It was midnight, and he was sobbing, "Brother Ed, I'm going to die!"

"Who said you were going to die?" I asked him. "Did you go to a doctor? Did a doctor say you were going to die?"

"No, no," he cried, "I just know I'm going to die."

I said, "You're not going to die. The devil's lying to you."

I stayed on the phone with him for an hour and a half, trying to get him to resist the devil's lie. He wouldn't resist it, and three days later, he killed himself.

People know if you believe the Word or not. Those dea-cons watched me go on with God when other men would have given up. So you're too late to talk me out of faith. You're too late to talk me out of my relationship with God. *I know faith works!* I've made mistakes, but I always get right back on track with the Word of God. It works! The Word of God will never fail!

Quit griping. Quit moaning. Quit complaining. You ought to thank God you've got a roof over your head, you're healthy, you're free, and you're alive. If you would start to count your blessings, you would find that you've got more blessings than problems.

Don't let the devil bring up your past to you. Remember, the Word says you've been made the righteousness of God.

"But Brother Dufresne, you don't know what I've been through!"

No, and I don't want to know. It's buried under the blood of Jesus Christ. The Bible says you're a new creature. You're a new *species.* You aren't that old man. So don't let the devil tell you, "You'll never amount to anything. You know what you did, you rotten person!"

The Late Ed Dufresne

"Oh, you're talking about that dead guy." That's what I tell the devil. "You're talking about the Ed Dufresne who gave his heart to Jesus and that old sin nature died in 1966. I'm the *new* Ed Dufresne."

If you had known me before I was saved, you wouldn't believe it. I was crazy! I carried a gun in my car. I spent my whole $55 paycheck to buy everyone a beer when my kids needed clothes. You're nuts if you do that. The devil's got you.

One day, there was a new guy on the job. He said, "Did you know that Jesus loves you?" He said not only did Jesus love me, but *he* loved me, too! I had never heard a man say he loved me.

I jumped back and said, "You're a queer!"

They put this guy with me as my partner! I didn't want him, because he went around speaking in tongues all day. He was a beat-up old ex-rodeo cowboy. He had rods in his arms and his legs. He was a rough, tough cowboy who could beat anyone up. But he got saved, because his old mother in New Mexico used to pray for him all the time.

My partner told me, "You need Jesus."

I went to the boss to complain. I said, "You gave me this holy roller. I've got to get away from him!" (I didn't know it was God dealing with me.)

Yet he wouldn't leave me alone. It gradually got into my heart that Jesus loved me. He didn't ask me to come to his church bake sale or anything; he just told me that Jesus loved me.

The Day Love Won

There was a day I couldn't take it any longer: I went to church with him the next Sunday morning. I wore an old white shirt that was still dirty from bar-hopping the night before. And I had a hangover.

Fifty people attended the church, and I thought they were very rude. As the announcements were being made, these people kept saying, "Amen." In the church I was raised in, you didn't say anything.

Then they started to sing, and they sang about the blood. All of a sudden, a Filipino woman stood up and gave a message in tongues. My eyeballs were bulging.

"My God — what's that?" I asked my partner. But I knew it was supernatural.

Then her husband got up and interpreted. I never did hear what that pastor said that morning. I knew I had to have what my partner had. When he gave the invitation — "Does anyone want to get saved?" — I ran right down to the altar, hangover and all. (Later, they told me they thought I'd run out the back door.)

Back then, churches had altars and altar benches. I knelt and said, "God, forgive me of my sins." The blood of Jesus Christ came out of heaven, and that little, skinny Ed Dufresne died! He melted right there. And when I came up, I was a new creature in Christ!

From that day on, I've been working for God, because that blood worked! That blood got all over my sins and washed them away! The old Ed Dufresne died.

When I had my church in Torrance, the people I used to run around with would sneak into the back of the church. They'd heard, "Ed Dufresne is down there pastoring!"

After they'd see me and hear me preach, they'd say to one another, "No, that ain't him. It *looks* like him, but that ain't him. The Ed Dufresne we knew was *crazy!*"

Crazy for God

Now I'm crazy for God. I've got a reputation, and I don't care. I'm on my way to heaven, and before I go, I'm going to take some people with me.

I know that the Word of God is true. You can't talk me out of it. You can tell me all kinds of things, but *I know the Word works!*

I've seen cancers fall off people's faces. I've seen the toughest old beer-guzzling drunken husbands come down and give their heart to Jesus and watch that blood wash them. I've seen people come up out of wheelchairs, walking.

If you don't know Jesus Christ as your personal Savior, you, too, can come to Him, and He will wash you with His blood. If you are a homosexual, God will forgive you of that, too. The blood of Jesus Christ will cleanse you. It will even take AIDS away, or any other disease. That blood — oh, the blood of Jesus!

Chapter 5

The Righteousness of God

Are you wearing your badge of authority? The authority you possess over the devil is the Name of Jesus.

Wearing your badge is actually another way of stating something you already know: You are to put on the whole armor of God and stand against the enemy. Do you know the whole armor of God includes the breastplate of righteousness?

In this chapter we want to look at being *righteousness*-conscious, not *sin*-conscious. If you never get the revelation knowledge that you are the righteousness of God, Satan will beat your brains out!

You can go to church every day of your life — and you *will* go to heaven — but you will live a defeated life on this earth until you have revelation knowledge that *you are the righteousness of God*.

What is "righteous"? Righteous means being in right standing with the Father.

Suppose someone gave you a house completely paid for, yet you didn't move into it until five years later. When did it become your house — when it was paid for, or when you moved into it? When it was paid for!

Two thousand years ago, Jesus paid for you to be in right standing with God. It wasn't anything you did; it's something *He* did. By His blood He gave you right standing before the heavenly Father. Just go ahead and move into it!

The Roots of a Bad Self-Image

I came out of a bad home environment. I didn't come out of a home where we were Christians, and where Mother and Dad loved one another, held hands, and kissed each other. We kids had to duck at the dinner table because spaghetti would go flying across the table and hit the wall! There was no love in our home.

I can understand why our prisons are so full today. I can understand why so many children are so unstable. They come out of homes like that.

Because I had that kind of a background, I was very withdrawn. I didn't have a good self-image. It took time, even after I got saved, to build that into me. In fact, it took *years* to get rid of my bad self-image.

It bothered me even after I went into the ministry. It was hard enough to get up and preach, much less give a testimony. I was intimidated by the other people on the platform. If I was in a convention and they said, "Brother Ed, come up here," they never know the fear that would hit me in my heart. I would think, "Oh, what have I got to say to them?"

At Campmeeting many times in Tulsa, Brother Kenneth E. Hagin would call me out, saying, "You've got something, Brother Ed."

I'd say, "No, no! I haven't got anything." But I knew I did, and so did he.

He would say, "It will be all right. Get up here." When I got up on the platform, the anointing would hit me, my mind would go "poof," I'd open my mouth, and God could take over. Praise God for fathers in the faith who have patience with people.

That bad self-image was trying to come back on me. Many of you have a hard time with it, too. It's because you've had that sin-consciousness in your life so long, and it's hard to turn that thing around. But you can do it with the Word of God!

The Worm Turned!

Another problem people face is that the devil gets preachers to build into you the idea that you're "nothing but a worm." I'm not a worm anymore; I'm a child of the King! A worm is the devil's bait — he likes worms — but *I'm* not a worm!

And I didn't even have to work for my salvation; it was already provided.

However, as James says, the devil would rob me of these things if he could keep me doubleminded. Let's look again at this scripture:

If any of you lack wisdom, let him ask of God, that giveth to all men liberally, and upbraideth not; and it shall be given him.

But let him ask in faith, nothing wavering. For he that wavereth is like a wave of the sea driven with the wind and tossed.

For let not that man think that he shall receive any thing of the Lord.

A double minded man in unstable in all his ways.

James 1:5-8

A two-spirited or doubleminded man says, "I'm the righteousness of God" one minute, and the next minute he says, "I'm nothing but a worm." He goes back and forth, and the Bible says he won't receive anything — *"But without faith it is impossible to please him"* (Hebrews 11:6). I didn't write that; God did!

Read the Instructions

So if things aren't working, we need to get back to the instructions — the Word — and find out what's wrong.

You macho men know what I mean. At Christmastime, when you buy a bike for your child, and you open the box and find the bike's in pieces, you don't bother to read the instructions. Oh, no, macho men know how to assemble a bicycle! But after you've got it all together, and you've got five or six bolts left over, *then* you go back to the instructions.

If things aren't working in your life, go back to the mastermind instructions, and find out *why* they aren't working. *Why* isn't your healing coming? *Why* aren't you being blessed financially? Something's wrong.

It isn't God's fault, because He already built our house of provision. He already gave us the deed. He already said, before we were even born, "Their righteousness is of Me." Just move into it!

From Nothing to Something

Jesus purchased our righteousness. He gave us right standing with God. I was nothing, but now I am something: I'm a child of the King! This isn't being egotistical; I'm just saying what the Bible says.

The Bible says, "Humble yourselves therefore under the mighty hand of God, that he may exalt you in due time" (1 Peter 5:6). If God says, "You are the righteousness of God," then I am the righteousness of God.

Never tell God, "O God, You know what a weak worm of the dust I am." He already knows that.

"And You know, Lord, that I am weak and unworthy. I'm a failure. O God, I'm such a black-hearted sinner." If you're born again, you don't pray this way. The more you talk about weakness and unworthiness, the more the devil will use it to get you to believe that you don't have any right to stand before the throne of God.

The Privileges of Sonship

We're raising our little boy with love and discipline. That boy is sweet! The other day, he crawled into the bathtub with me, kissed me on the neck, and said, Daddy, I love you so much!"

I just about came unglued! I felt like saying, "What do you want? I'll give you *anything!*" You parents know what I'm talking about.

Stephen knows where he belongs. If we would try to lock him out of the house, he would beat the door down and tear the windows out to get back in. Our house is where he belongs.

He never says, "Oh, I'm such a worm! Dad, Mom, can I *please* have some food out of the refrigerator?" Are you kidding me? We keep cartons of ice cream on hand, because we get all the neighbor kids at our house, and we tell them about Jesus. They all come right in and help themselves to that ice cream.

Stephen doesn't come and beg for it. He knows he's in right standing with his mother and father. He knows that we love him, that we care about him, and he has a right to what we have.

He just walks in the house, says, "Come on" to the kids, and they all go marching to the refrigerator. Stephen helps himself — sometimes to two bowls.

And I don't care. Ice cream is cheap. I'd rather have all the kids at my house instead of being an old grouch who runs them off, yelling, "Oh, get out of here!" That's the way so many parents do to them. Praise God, they can come to our house, where there's an atmosphere of love.

Go Boldly Into Your Father's House

God has said, "Let us therefore come boldly unto the throne of grace, that we may obtain mercy, and find grace to help in time of need" (Hebrews 4:16).

Some of you are not there yet, because it doesn't happen overnight. *You've got to renew your mind with the Word of God until you know who you are in Christ.*

Don't say, "Oh, I don't know if God will heal me." The devil wants to keep you trapped in sin-consciousness. You must rebuke him!

51

There are a lot of churches where the devil uses the pastor's preaching to keep the people in poverty all their life. Yes, they're good people and, yes, they're all going to heaven — I didn't say they're not — but they are walking far beneath their privileges, and they have not taken what has already been deeded to them as Christians.

I'm not letting anyone talk me out of the fact that I'm in right standing with my Father!

"Well, Brother Dufresne, you make mistakes."

The Promise of Forgiveness

Yes, I've had a lot of people point out my mistakes, but you've got to realize that none of us are perfect, except through the blood of Jesus Christ. That's not a license to go out and sin, but when I do make a mistake, the blood of Jesus Christ cleanses me of all unrighteousness.

A man who isn't righteous can't be *un*righteous, because he's a sinner. Therefore, this passage in Hebrews is addressed to those who once were righteous, but then became *un*righteous because of sin. God said He will forgive us of all unrighteousness if we will simply ask him. That's what right standing is all about.

Some of you stayed away from church when you made a mistake. You were ashamed, but that's nothing but the devil. You have to run right back to church and go down to the altar. Those people love you. Admit, "I made a mistake," and praise God for the blood of Jesus. Tell the devil, *"Take your hands off my stuff!"*

An Example of Forgiveness and Restoration

Here's an illustration of how Christ has given us righteousness and wisdom.

Years ago, when I was going to junior high school, I used to work on a chicken farm. I was the person who cleaned the manure from underneath the cages, loaded it in a wheelbarrow, and put it in a big stack. I also slaughtered the chickens. I did *everything* around that farm. For this I got 75 cents an hour!

My boss, Mr. Goodwin, loved me very much. He was just like a dad to me. When my own mom and dad would go on drunks, he would just love on me. And I loved him very much.

But then something happened. Every once in a while, a man who worked in another part of the farm would come into the incubator area where I was feeding the little chicks. Before I knew it, he was coming once a day. He would say, "You know, Mr. Goodwin is cheap. As a matter of fact, he ought to give you more money, considering how much work you do." He started putting all these thoughts into my mind against Mr. Goodwin.

Finally I joined in. You'd better watch out who you run around with! If they've got a wrong spirit about them, it'll get on you if you listen. They'll start talking against your pastor, and before you know it, you'll be talking against your pastor. That's what happened to me. I got caught up in talking against Mr. Goodwin. I wasn't saved then, of course.

Mr. Goodwin had a little workshop next to the incubator room. The cracks in the walls were wide enough for him to hear what was being said in the next room. He was in his workshop one day when this worker came to see me. And we started roasting Mr. Goodwin. I'll never forget when Mr. Goodwin walked into that incubator room!

He looked right at me. He said, "So you think this and you think I'm that..." And right away I tried to defend myself. He said, "Is that the way you feel?"

I said, "That's right."

He said, "You're fired!"

Of course, he fired the other man, too.

I walked out of there, but I tell you, something in me let me know I was wrong. I felt so bad.

Two weeks went by, and Mr. Goodwin's son came over to my house, knocked on my door, and said, "Ed, my dad loves you with all his heart. All you have to do is go down to the store and ask him to forgive you."

And I did. I got on my bicycle, rode down there, and said, "Mr. Goodwin, would you please forgive me for what I said? I didn't really mean it. I said it, but I didn't really mean it."

The Benefits of Repentance

"Well, I know you got to talking to the other guy," he said. "You've got your job back. Besides that, I'm giving you $1.25 an hour. And besides that, you're going to be a manager over this building."

Think about that! What did he do? He made me more than right standing. He gave me more than I was getting before. And that's what God does for us when we make mistakes and come to Him and repent!

After that, I didn't have to shovel you-know-what anymore. What I *deserved* was to have been out there another five years shoveling manure! But because I went to Mr. Goodwin and asked for forgiveness, he got tears in his eyes and he forgave me. He brought me back and gave me more than I had before: better pay and a better job. I'll never forget Mr. Goodwin. His example of forgiveness has always burned in me.

And that's the way God is to His children! You can make mistakes — you can blow it — but, praise God, you've been made the righteousness of God, and that's what righteous means.

When you come to Christ, He cleans you up and makes you right standing. He takes those old clothes of sin off you and puts new clothes of righteousness back on you.

How God Sees Our Flaws

I'm not a quitter, but there was a time in my life when I said, "I'm not worthy to be in the ministry."

The devil was right: I wasn't worthy. Things had happened, and God dealt with me. I'll never forget it. I said, "Lord, I've got so many flaws."

Do you know what He did? He gave me a mini-vision one day — just a little vision. He showed me a statue of myself, and He showed me it had cracks in it.

I said, "That's what I'm trying to tell You — I'm full of flaws." I tried to blame it on my childhood, reasoning, "Well, Lord, if I had been raised in a Christian home, maybe I'd be a better preacher. Maybe certain things would never have happened to me." We use everything as an excuse.

All of a sudden, I saw blood coming out of those cracks! The Lord said, "The blood covers all your mistakes, even to the day that you die or Jesus comes, and you're made perfect like Him."

Meanwhile, we're not perfect like Him. We will make mistakes while we are still in this world. That's what the blood is all about — to forgive us of our sins and our unrighteousness. So quit harping on your mistakes!

The Power of the Blood

The Lord also told me that if you get into trouble and everything is taken away from you — your home and everything else — God will restore everything that the cankerworm steals from you (Joel 2:25), because He has made you in right standing with Himself, as if you had never sinned. In God's eyes, you're just like Adam was before he sinned. Did you know that's how powerful the blood is?

The cleansing blood of Jesus extends to the worst harlot in the street, to the dope addict, to the meanest, filthiest spirit people get into, such as homosexuality. All these sinners have to say is, "God forgive me," and that blood will cleanse them from their sin and give them right standing with God!

Many Christians won't have anything to do with God even after they're saved, but in God's eyes they're just as clean as if they had never sinned. He doesn't even *know* they sinned. He no longer has a record of it in heaven!

The devil's the one who has the record, and he'll try to entice you into sin-consciousness. He'll say, "Your parents never loved you."

You can reply, "Yes, but God loved me. And, yes, my parents did love me. They were just in bondage themselves."

Resist the Devil

We've got to deal with the devil. Instead of *agreeing* with him, saying, "Yeah, that's right — I'm no good," we've got to *resist* him. James told us to resist the devil and he would flee from us (James 4:7).

It's sad, but there are preachers who get up in their pulpits every Sunday and put that sense of sin-consciousness on their people, and the people go out of there feeling so beaten down and unworthy. I'd rather go to a John Wayne movie than go to one of those churches! At least you know John Wayne's the one wearing the white hat, which means he's the good guy, and he's going to win.

In some of those churches, you don't know who's going to win — the devil or God. Most of the time, it's the devil who's winning in those churches! But I want you to know that the devil isn't going to win. Read the back of the Book: We win!

The devil tells me all the time, "You're not *worthy* to be in the ministry." I used to get on a self-pity kick when he said that. We all like to have our little pity parties. The cure is realizing the love of Jesus.

It's like when Mr. Goodwin took me back. One minute I was out on the street because of my transgression, my sin. But it took just a minute for me to say, "I'm sorry," and for him to reinstate me with a promotion to manager and a 50-cent-an-hour raise. Bam! I was right back in my former job, and I was able to afford a motor scooter. I was in hog heaven!

But sometimes the effects of sin linger on in our lives, even though God has forgiven us of those sins. The effects of sin, such as a child born out of wedlock, are things we have to deal with for the rest of our lives.

Part of the Family of God

We're bringing up our son Stephen in an atmosphere of love and discipline. When he walks into our house, he knows it belongs to him as part of our family. That's exactly what God did to me when He saved me: I became a part of His family, with all the resulting privileges.

Let's look at some of the things that belong to us as part of the family of God:

> **Therefore take no thought, saying, What shall we eat? or, What shall we drink? or, Wherewithal shall we be clothed?**
>
> **(For after all these things do the Gentiles seek:) for your heavenly Father knoweth that ye have need of all these things.**
>
> **But seek ye first the kingdom of God, and his righteousness; [or right standing with God] and all these things shall be added unto you.**
>
> **Matthew 6:31-33**

This passage is talking about things — or as kids would say — "stuff." When you are conscious of your right standing with God, all these *things* will be *added to* you, not *subtracted from* you. How many of you know that if your daddy is a millionaire, and if you're in right standing with your daddy, that's yours, too?

The reason why things are being subtracted from you is because you're not walking in your righteousness. Righteousness is something you put on. Paul says, "Put on the whole armour of God, that ye may be able to stand against the wiles of the devil" (Ephesians 6:11). And one of the parts of that armor is "the breastplate of righteousness" (verse 14).

How Righteousness Protects You

The way the Lord showed it to me is, the breastplate of righteousness covers where your vital organs are. You need to walk in righteousness to protect yourself. If you don't, the devil will steal from you. He will steal your "stuff"!

And he will bring up all kinds of accusations against you in that mind of yours. That's why Paul said:

Casting down imaginations, and every high thing that exalteth itself against the knowledge of God....

2 Corinthians 10:5

The devil will tell you that you're no good, you're rotten, you're too big, you're too skinny, you've got a handicap, you've got this, you've got that. He'll bring up all these things and more.

When he tries it on me, I tell him, "No, I've been made the righteousness of God. The blood of Jesus is even in my flaws!" When you've been cleansed by the blood of Jesus, it's just like you never did anything wrong in God's eyes.

You see, *the biggest battlefield is in your mind.* When those darts, those imaginations, come to your mind, you must grab them and cast them down. You battle them by saying, "I *am* worthy. I have been made worthy by the blood of Jesus!" Use the Word of God against those thoughts and imaginations.

Some people feel too unworthy to even come to church meetings! They feel like they don't belong there. You *do* belong in church. If you've been saved, and God told you to go to a certain church, that is your church. It isn't just the pastor's church. It isn't just your friend's church. It's *your* church, too. You have a right to be there.

Opposed by Men

You'd be surprised how many churches ran me off before the faith message became popular. The Full Gospel church where I got saved rejected me and gave me "the left foot of fellowship" when I began preaching about divine healing.

In one church I occassionally preached in, the pastor left the church, and the deacons took the church over, and there was a church split within two weeks because of those power-hungry deacons.

I told them on the phone, "I'm not going to allow you to destroy these people. I'm coming to deal with you!" They phoned another man of God and said, "Ed's coming here to get us."

He said, "Good! I hope he gets you real good!"

When I got there, no one would pick me up at the airport. I had to get a taxi. Two weeks before, when I was there to preach, they had sent a limousine to pick me up.

I was walking in the prophet's anointing that morning. I told those deacons "guarding" the door, "In the Name of Jesus, move aside! You aren't tearing this church up!" I pushed them aside, walked in, went behind the curtains, and walked out and sat on the platform. When the rest of the deacons saw me sitting up there, they were running all over the place!

You've got to be bold to do that, but my knees were shaking. I got the situation turned around somewhat because the people and their former pastor loved me.

Walking in Righteousness

You have been made the righteousness of God. When some of you hear or read that statement, your minds go, "No, no!" That's nothing but the devil lying to you.

I don't make that statement in arrogance. I mean that, in sweetness yet in boldness, you are the righteousness of God. You don't need to sit around and rehash your past mistakes all day long.

You don't need to keep saying, "Well, I had five wives, and none of my marriages worked out." You don't need to say,

"Well, I had this problem and I had that problem." You don't need to say, "Oh, I was a terrible woman. I sold my body."

That woman died. That old sin nature was crucified with Christ. You're clean. You're pure. Maybe people don't see it, but you're clean and pure in God's eyes if you've been washed with the blood of Jesus Christ. People may talk about your past, but God doesn't talk about it. As a matter of fact, you're cleaner than the gossipers in the church!

You've got to walk in your righteousness to defeat the devil; to keep him from touching your stuff.

The subject of righteousness is one of the major areas where the devil beats Christians down. Many sermons are preached on it, adding to a believer's sense of unworthiness and sin-consciousness.

However, the fact that you have been made the righteousness of God does not give you license, or permission, to go out and sin, using the excuse, "Well, I'll be forgiven." I hope you've got enough sense not to do that.

God knows your heart. If you do sin and truly repent, God will restore you to right standing, just like Mr. Goodwin restored me.

Established in Righteousness

Notice Isaiah 54:14:

In righteousness shalt thou be established....

What does "establish" mean? It means "to be stable, to make firm, to settle the fact." Some of you need to quit messing around and establish a church home for yourself. Decide, "This is my church. This is where I will plant my finances. I'm part of this family. This is where I'm staying."

The Bible tells us not to forsake the assembling of ourselves together (Hebrews 10:25). People use many excuses because they don't want to assemble together. Don't forget, a doubleminded man — a two-spirited man — is unstable in all of his ways, and he won't receive anything from God.

As we see the world becoming darker and darker, we should want to come together in the house of God all the more, because the church where you worship is really your family of righteousness. It is your haven, your protection, your family — and everyone needs a family. So joining yourself to a church family will help establish you.

Battling Oppression and Fear

Isaiah 54:14 continues, "thou shalt be far from oppression." If you are oppressed, that means you need to get back and establish the fact of who you are in Christ. That will run the oppression off.

If things aren't working in my life, I go to God and say, "Lord, forgive me. Where am I missing it? I know that You're not withholding anything from me. Either I'm praying amiss, there's sin in my life, or there's a bad attitude in my life. Whatever it is, I want You to show me."

Verse 14 concludes, "thou shalt be far from oppression; for thou shalt not fear; and from terror; for it shall not come near thee."

Do you have fear in your life? Fear is unbelief. Fear is the opposite of faith. So if you've got fear in your life, you need to get back in step and work on running that fear out of your life.

Let me put it this way: If you work on the truth that you are righteous with God — if you can get that settled and established in your life — you won't have much trouble with your faith.

You'd be surprised how many Christians who sit in sin-consciousness churches are bitter against God. Just go to a funeral in one of those churches. You'll hear, "The Lord giveth and the Lord taketh away."

A 5-year-old boy sitting there hearing that, viewing the casket, is thinking, "My family wants me to go to church and serve their God, but He killed my mommy."

Do you wonder why your children get turned off from church? It's because you sit around the dinner table and have the preacher for dinner. The reason why preachers' kids run off and don't want anything to do with the ministry is because their parents sat around the dinner table and talked about all the people who were coming against them and all the other problems in the church.

You go to church on Sunday morning, saying, "Yes, I believe in healing," but you're popping pain pills and lecturing your children, "Now don't you get on drugs, kids." I'm glad God's not doubleminded.

We're still not completely perfect at it, but we're careful not to talk about problems in front of our little boy. We don't want him to be turned off to Jesus.

The Power of Righteousness

"For thou shalt not fear; and...terror...shall not come near thee."

What does the prophet Isaiah mean by the phrase "near thee"? He means terror won't come near the righteousness of God. So if you've got your breastplate of righteousness on, it isn't just a tin breastplate; it's something you wear and walk in every day. That's being righteousness-conscious.

Jesus did it. He stood in front of Lazarus' tomb and said, "Father, I thank You that You already heard Me." *When* did God hear Jesus? Four days before when, upon hearing of Lazarus' sickness, Jesus responded, "This sickness is not unto death...."

You see, Jesus walked in His right standing. When you pray, believing that you receive, that's it! Then you are to start to praise Him, saying, "Thank You, Lord. I thank You that our rent is paid."

Jesus was righteous, and the Bible says a righteous man's prayer avails much (James 5:16). There is much power behind a righteous man's prayer — not an unbeliever's prayer, and not a worm's prayer, but a *righteous* man's prayer.

A righteous man's prayer is, "Father, I thank You that You already heard me."

Righteousness is something that you not only wear and walk in; it's something you've got to renew. I have to reestablish my sense of righteousness all the time. When those guilt feelings return for what I did years and years ago, before I was saved, I have to say, "No, wait a minute, devil. You aren't going to put that on me!"

Winning Your War

Now go to verse 15:

Behold, they shall surely gather together [and war against you], **but not by me: whosoever shall gather together against thee** [the righteousness of God] **shall fall for thy** [righteousness'] **sake.**

What is it that shall gather against you? *Trouble.*

Verse 17:

No weapon that is formed against thee [the righteousness of God] **shall prosper; and every tongue that shall rise against thee** [the righteousness of God] **in judgment thou shalt condemn. This is the heritage of the servants of the Lord, and their righteousness is of me, saith the Lord.**

Walk in Your Inheritance

Determine to renew your mind. Realize that you have a right to all the promises of God. God is no respecter of persons. I've learned to walk in what belongs to me. What belongs to God is *my* inheritance!

If your father died and an outsider tried to get some of that inheritance, it would make you so mad, you'd almost leave your salvation at the door and go fight him, wouldn't you?

Why don't you fight that way for what belongs to you in God — for your inheritance in God? He has promised you healing. He has said all your needs would be met in the Name of Jesus. And He has said that if you believe on the

Lord Jesus Christ, your children, or your household, will all be saved (Acts 11:14; 16:31).

My family are coming in. I've been in the ministry 25 years. (As soon as I got saved, I was in the ministry; the ministry of helps.)

Right before my alcoholic mother died, she received Christ over the telephone, went into her bedroom, lay down, and died. They found her the next day.

God told me the reason He took her was because she had a weak mind, yet she had confessed Jesus as the Lord of her life. He said, "I let her come home right then." He knew she was weak. He told me she is in Smith Wigglesworth's class and the classes of other well-known preachers up in heaven. If you're a baby Christian and you go to glory, you'll get educated up there.

If some of your children aren't going the right way, if they're not serving God, if they're on dope — whatever the problem is — cast that care on the Lord.

Stand on the Word of God for their salvation. Believe God, because you have covenant rights as His child. *The blood covenant Jesus cut with the Father is your inheritance.*

Whatever problem you are facing, you have a covenant with your Father. Find out what He says about your inheritance. Go read the will He left, the Old and New Testaments, and make sure that you get everything that His will promises you.

Chapter 6
The Accuser of the Brethren

And I heard a loud voice saying in heaven, Now is come salvation, and strength, and the kingdom of our God, and the power of his Christ: for the accuser of our brethren is cast down, which accused them before our God day and night.

Revelation 12:10

One day as I was reading my Bible, the word "accuser" kept coming to me. The Lord said, "Look up that word in your concordance." I discovered "accuser" means "an opponent in a lawsuit."

The opponent we Christians face is the devil, the accuser of the brethren. It is important that we learn to recognize his tactics. How else will we know how to come against our enemy if we don't know who he is or what he's doing?

In this chapter, I am going to show you something from the Word of God about our enemy that has helped me be victorious over him, and I trust it will do the same for you.

To begin with, look at the following scripture:

My people are destroyed for lack of knowledge: because thou hast rejected knowledge, I will also reject thee, that thou shalt be no priest to me: seeing thou hast forgotten the law of thy God, I will also forget thy children.

Hosea 4:6

Robbed by the Accuser

Christians have been robbed of their rights because of lack of knowledge of the Word of God! For example, some people have said, "God killed my baby." That is a *lie* from the pit of hell! God did *not* kill your baby! You were *robbed from* and *destroyed* because of a lack of knowledge of God's Word and God's commandments.

Jesus Himself said:

The thief cometh not, but for to steal, and to kill, and to destroy: I am come that they might have life, and that they might have it more abundantly.

John 10:10

God wants you to live a good 70 years and then some.

If someone were to tell you that God took your child to heaven because He needed him, I would ask you, "Do you think God needs babies to fly around with little wings on and carry messages?" *No!*

Babies are not angels. If a naked baby flew up to me on little wings, I would tell him to go away, for many of God's angels are nine feet tall! God has plenty of angels to serve Him in heaven. God needs babies *down here* to grow up and preach the Word. The Word doesn't need to be preached in heaven.

Tradition vs. the Word

Certain ideas have been planted in Christians' minds by religious tradition down through the years. And people perish because of lack of knowledge of God's *Word!* When you get into the Word, however, you'll find out how to come against our opponent, the accuser of the brethren, and be set free!

According to Webster's Dictionary, a lawsuit is "a suit in law: a case before a court." Our enemy, our lawsuitor, is constantly trying to slap a lawsuit on you before the Father — and if he can prove you are in the wrong, you will have to pay the penalty.

So picture, if you will, God in heaven on His throne, Jesus sitting at His right hand, and the devil down here accusing you. Doesn't that look like a scene in a courtroom?

God Has To Keep His Word

This may startle you, but God is a just God concerning both the devil and you. He will not allow one person to sin and get away with it while another sins and gets caught. God is no respecter of persons. The Word says,

God is not a man, that he should lie....

Numbers 23:19

He *has* to keep His Word.

You need to realize that the accuser of the brethren comes before the Father day and night, trying to pin something on you. There are many ways he can come against you. However, the Word will show you how to win those battles with the accuser of the brethren, that old enemy, Satan.

Jesus' Example

Jesus said in John 14:30, "Hereafter I will not talk much with you: for the prince of this world cometh, and hath nothing in me."

When Jesus came to earth, He walked under the Abrahamic Covenant, just as the Old Testament prophets did. He was tempted just like you and I are (Hebrews 4:15), but Satan, the prince of this world, had nothing in Him — found no fault or sin in Him — because Jesus walked in God's commandments.

You may argue, "Yes, but Jesus was the Son of God."

Who do you think *you* are? Jesus is your Big Brother, and you became a son of God through Him. Although Jesus is Deity, the Son of God, He laid aside all of His glory and divine privileges (Philippians 2:5-8) and came to earth to live as a man.

Jesus walked on the earth in a body like ours, He was tempted like we are, and He conquered Satan! Satan tried to put a lawsuit on Jesus, but he could not. Jesus said, "He has nothing in me."

When Satan attacked Him, Jesus replied, "It is written..." (Luke 4:1-13). Jesus always quoted the Word of God to the accuser of the brethren!

The Christian's Unique Authority

God did not reveal Satan to the Jews of the Old Testament as He has to believers under the New Testament. Those who lived under the Old Testament did not have the authority we have today, because Jesus had not yet come to earth. It is because of what Jesus accomplished on the cross that Christians can take authority over Satan.

People under the Old Testament had to walk under the "umbrella" of the Old Covenant for protection. If they got out from under that umbrella, the devil nailed them.

Notice that the men who wrote the Old Testament did not mention much about Satan. You will find a little about him in the Book of Isaiah and also in the Book of Job, but not much revelation was given about him otherwise. As a result, God was blamed for a lot of things that were not His fault!

The Christian's Lawyer

We New Testament Christians have a Lawyer who stands before the Father on our behalf. His name is Jesus! He is our Advocate. He is there to plead our case. The enemy has nothing on Jesus, and Jesus is pleading *our* case. *We,* through Jesus, have the authority to bring the Word of God to bear against the enemy before he can even get us into the courtroom!

Jesus of Nazareth had every opportunity to have an unforgiving attitude toward the people who crucified Him. He had every opportunity to get into strife. He could have become angry and called all the angels in heaven to wipe out the whole mob. He had the power to do it, but He didn't.

When He hung on the cross, they said there was *no deceit* in His mouth. Jesus remained in forgiveness and in the love walk throughout His life and ministry here on earth. That is why He could say, "Satan has nothing in me." The Bible says that Jesus did not have "ought against any." That means that He didn't hold a grudge against anyone. And that is why He could say, "Satan has nothing in me."

Do You Have "Ought Against Any"?

If you are a "faith person," you probably can quote the entire passage of Mark 11:22-24, but can you quote verses 25 and 26? The promises found in Mark 11:22-24 will not work for believers if they do not fulfill the Word in verses 25 and 26. Let's look at these verses.

> And when ye stand praying, forgive, if ye have ought against any: that your Father also which is in heaven may forgive you your trespasses.
>
> But if ye do not forgive, neither will your Father which is in heaven forgive your trespasses.

Suppose you are coming against a big mountain — a mountain of sickness. You want to blow that mountain down with your faith, but it refuses to move. What's wrong? Read Mark 11:25,26 again; you may find your answer there: "...when ye stand praying, forgive...that your Father...in heaven may forgive your trespasses."

God cannot go against His Word. If He went over that boundary and answered your prayer when you had unforgiveness in your heart, Satan could nail Him. God would be a liar if He went beyond His word, and of course He won't do that.

If you are not operating in the Word of God, Satan has a legal right to go before the Father and put a lawsuit on you. But he does not have that right if you are standing on the Word and living by its precepts.

Suppose you own a restaurant, and a man comes into your restaurant and slips or falls down. He may try to sue you, and it is legal for him to do so if he can prove that his accident was caused by your negligence. If he can prove you were at fault, he will win the case against you. But if you have been careful to adhere to all safety regulations, the court will not find you are to blame, and you will win the case.

Do Everything the Word Says

It is the same in your Christian life. Don't be negligent in doing what the Word says. Then the accuser of the brethren will have no case against you when he stands day and night before God, accusing you. He will have nothing in you.

If you are operating in unforgiveness, God cannot answer your prayers. That is all there is to it. You can shout, yell, speak in tongues, and listen to tapes by all the greatest speakers — but it won't do you a bit of good unless you walk in forgiveness and love, and do what the Word of God tells you to do.

Likewise, ye younger, submit yourselves unto the elder. Yea, all of you be subject one to another, and be clothed with humility: for God resisteth the proud, and giveth grace to the humble.

Humble yourselves therefore under the mighty hand of God, that he may exalt you in due time.

1 Peter 5:5,6

The Word Exalts

God doesn't want you to exalt yourself. But if you will humble yourself to the Word of God and promote the Word, *the Word of God will promote you.* If you are preaching what the Word says, you will be exalted along with the Word.

The Word will promote you out of sickness!

The Word will promote you out of poverty!

The Word will promote you out of loneliness!

The Word will promote you out of fear!

Promote the Word of God, and in due time the accuser of the brethren won't be able to touch you. Why? He will have nothing in you, because you are following Jesus' example of walking in love and the Word.

Casting All Your Care on Him

Casting all your care upon him; for he careth for you.

Be sober, be vigilant; because your adversary the devil, as a roaring lion, walketh about, seeking whom he may devour.

1 Peter 5:7,8

Have you ever been around a "religious" person? "Religious" people have a religious spirit, and they can't even talk sense. They say they can "believe" for anything, but they really can't believe for a pair of socks!

The above text says that your adversary the devil, as a roaring lion, walks around seeking whom he *may* devour. The word "may" means that he *might* be able to devour you *if you allow him to do so.*

The word "adversary" means in the Greek "an opponent in a lawsuit." Let's read our text this way: "Be sober, be watchful, because your opponent in a lawsuit, the devil, is going around seeking whom he may slap a lawsuit on."

Natural Protection Against the Devil

Many people are going around doing the devil's work. If they see a brand-new luxury car, they think, "I'll let the driver of that car run into me, and I'll sue." Sometimes they even stage a fake accident. This is one of the reasons why we must have insurance.

Some Christians get so excited about faith that they say, "Well, I'm not going to buy any insurance. *I'm* going to live by faith!" Go ahead, but I, for one, am going to be *sober-minded* and keep my insurance. In most states, it is now a *law* that if you operate a car, you must have insurance, and we should abide by the laws of the land.

This is not to put the faith message down — I am a faith man myself — I just want to encourage you to remain sober-minded and watchful that you walk according to the Word of God.

You don't need to be so fearful that you're always on the lookout for the devil. You can't see him anyway, unless you have the gift of discerning of spirits. God means for you to be watchful and sober-minded about His Word — and He also wants you to cast all your care on Him.

Satan is the opponent in a lawsuit, the accuser of the brethren, your adversary. He goes about as a roaring lion, making a big noise to scare you. However, there is no action behind that big noise *unless* he can put a lawsuit on you.

Satan cannot touch you if you are walking in the Word of God. If you are walking in forgiveness and the love walk of harmony and agreement, you can get the case against you thrown out of court. However, if you operate in unforgiveness, you are tying the hands of Jesus, and you will lose the case Satan brings against you.

Healing Is for You

Understand that *God does not want you sick.* Many people do not want to hear that statement, because they enjoy sympathy and self-pity — but that stuff will kill you!

I'll never forget the time when I was beginning to understand the truths of divine healing from the Word of God. I heard an evangelist by the name of Kenneth Copeland preach in Denver, Colorado, that it is God's will for us to be healed.

Then my daughter Stephanie became ill with a raging fever. It continued even after taking her to the doctor. I went into her room and said, "Either the Word is true, or it is not true!" Satan had nothing in me. I checked my life: There was nothing. I had *the right* to receive healing for my daughter. I had that right because of what Jesus did for me two thousand years ago. I had the right to act on the Word of God.

I reasoned that if it was not God's will to heal my little girl, He should never have written it in the New Testament, and He should never have put all those diseases on Jesus. That would have been a miscarriage of justice.

In the Driver's Seat

Let's rightly divide the Word. Because of what Jesus did when He died on the cross, was buried, and was resurrected from the dead, *New Testament Christians are in the driver's seat!* That means if the devil tries to put something on you, *you* can run him off.

I got mad at the devil that night my daughter was so ill. I got some oil and dumped it all over her! I quoted all the scriptures I had learned concerning healing, and I declared, "As far as I am concerned, she is *healed!* The Word works! If it doesn't, I'm going to forget it and go back to the bars. I'm tired of 'playing church.' Either the Word works or it doesn't!"

Twenty minutes went by. The devil said, "She's dead for sure — and *you're* going to be tried for manslaughter!"

I said, "By His stripes she was healed!"

Around 10 o'clock little Stephanie climbed out of her crib and tore the house up until 2 o'clock in the morning, *completely healed!* I had cast my care upon God. His Word works!

The *King James Version* translates it, "Casting all your care upon him; for he careth for you."

Worry is a *sin.* Worry is operating in *fear* — and fear is the opposite of *faith.*

Poor Old Job

Many people lament, "Poor old Job! I must be like Job." I said that once myself. I'd had a tooth pulled, and my gums became swollen and infected. I was going around dizzy from pain pills, moaning, "I'm *just like* Job! God is going to teach me something out of this big swollen place on the side of my mouth."

I did learn something: I learned not to allow the devil to put a lawsuit on me!

There was a man in the land of Uz whose name was Job; and that man was blameless and upright, and one who (reverently) feared God and abstained from and shunned evil [because it was wrong].

And there were born to him seven sons and three daughters.

He possessed seven thousand sheep, three thousand camels, five hundred yoke of oxen, five hundred female donkeys, and a very great body of servants, so that this man was the greatest of all the men of the east.

Job 1:1-3 *The Amplified Bible*

Although Job was a rich man, and the greatest man in the East, he was a *worrier!* After his sons and daughters had gathered for birthday feasts at each other's homes, Job would rise up early the next morning and send for them to purify and hallow them. He offered burnt offerings for all of them. The Bible does not state that they *had* sinned, but Job *suspected* that they had.

He said, "It may be that my sons have sinned, and cursed or disowned God in their hearts. Thus did Job at all [such] times" (verses 4 and 5).

Worrying Over Wayward Children

Do you roll and toss all night when your wayward or unsaved children are out? Worry, worry, worry! Do you say, "I wonder if my baby is out with that kid again?" If you do, you are operating in *fear*, and your angels have to step back and fold their arms. There is no way they can do anything to protect your children.

You should have more faith than that. You should be confessing, "My children are disciples taught of the Lord. I have brought them up in the ways of the Lord, and they shall not depart from it. They will know right from wrong."

As you operate in *faith* and speak words of faith over them, God will jerk the slack out of them, and no one will be able to harm them.

Fear Brings Satan

Now there was a day when the sons [the angels] of God came to present themselves before the Lord, so Satan — the adversary and accuser — also came among them.

And the Lord said to Satan, From where did you come? Then Satan answered the Lord, From going to and fro on the earth, and walking up and down on it.

And the Lord said to Satan, Have you considered My servant Job, that there is none like him on the earth, a blameless and upright man, one who (reverently) fears God and abstains from and shuns evil [because it is wrong]?

Job 1:6-8 The Amplified Bible

Notice that God made a good confession over Job. But He knew that Job was operating in fear. *Fear will bring Satan on the scene every time,* for he has been cast down from heaven, and he goes to and fro like a roaring lion, seeking whom he may devour. That is why you have to fight fear like a rattlesnake, using the Word of God against him.

If you are experiencing oppression or depression in your life, it means you have fear in your life, and you need to drive it out with the Word of God.

Then Satan answered the Lord, Does Job (reverently) fear God for nothing?

Have You not put a hedge about him and his house and all that he has, on every side? You have conferred prosperity and happiness upon him in the work of his hands, and his possessions have increased in the land.

But put forth Your hand now, and touch all that he has, and he will curse You to Your face.

Job 1:9-11

Job himself let down the hedge that protected him because he walked in fear instead of faith. As a result, God no

longer had a legal right to protect him. *Job* was the one who
allowed the accuser of the brethren to slap a lawsuit on him.

If you go around saying, "I'm just like poor old Job. I'm
suffering for God. God is testing me," you need to read James
1:13. God tempts no man. And God wasn't tempting Job.
God was the same in Job's time as He was in New Testament
times and as He is today.

Job's Victory

When you read the ending of the Book of Job, you will
find that Job got out of fear and back on faith. He got forgiveness in his heart toward those knuckleheads who were
running around with him and blaming God for all that had
happened to him.

Once you read the Book of Job in that light, it will
change your whole outlook. For example, verse 10 of the last
chapter reads:

**And the Lord turned the captivity of Job, when he prayed
for his friends; also the Lord gave Job twice as much as he
had before.**

If you want to be like Job and get your fortunes restored,
you must get rid of that unforgiving spirit and straighten
your life out. After you do this, still following Job's example,
you will also get healed and prosper like Job did!

Chapter 7
The Weapons Satan Uses Against You

There are some clauses in the Word of God that Satan will try to use to get you into a spiritual court and slap a lawsuit on you.

In this chapter, we will cover some of these clauses, because they will affect you in every area of your life: spiritual, physical, and financial. However, if you will learn how to operate in the love of God and in the Word, Satan won't have an opportunity to come against you.

Clause 1: Unforgiveness

And whenever you stand praying, if you have anything against any one, forgive him and let it drop — leave it, let it go — in order that your Father Who is in heaven may also forgive you your [own] failings and shortcomings and let them drop.

Mark 11:25 *The Amplified Bible*

Have you said concerning someone, "I'm not going to forgive that old man. You just don't know what he did to me!" And there you are, suffering from arthritis, heart trouble, hardening of the arteries, and so forth.

You will die of those problems before your time because of that unforgiveness in your heart. And there is nothing that our heavenly Father can do about it, because He is a just God, and He must keep His Word!

"And when ye stand praying, forgive...that your Father also which is in heaven may forgive your trespasses."

Let's suppose you are asking the Father, in the Name of Jesus, for your healing. Jesus, your Lawyer, is up in heaven interceding for you, pleading your case. The accuser of the brethren is daily accusing you.

Your prayer comes before the Father. Satan jumps up and yells, "Wait a minute! You say in your Word, 'When you stand praying, forgive.' This person has unforgiveness against Brother So-and-so. You can't answer his prayer!"

Because of your unforgiveness, Jesus can do nothing. And God has to say, "That's right. I cannot go against my Word"

But it's not too late! You can still get forgiveness in your heart toward that person. Then your Advocate can say, "Wait a minute! Let Me quote that same verse back to you, Satan. Yes, Mark 11:25 says, 'When ye stand praying, forgive...,' but my client forgave that woman at 11:59 p.m." Then He will add, "Father, grant his healing," and it will be done for you.

Clause 2: Withholding Your Tithes From God

I don't want you to get into condemnation, but unforgiveness and strife go along with not paying your tithes.

You may say, "Yes, but Galatians 3:13 tells us that Jesus became a curse for us. He did away with the curse of the Law." Since when was tithing a curse of the Law? Abraham paid tithes to Melchizedek *before* the Law was given!

God said in His Word, "My people perish for lack of knowledge." If you are perishing financially, you need to get into His Word and see what you are doing that prevents you from prospering.

No, God doesn't *need* your tithes, but *you* need to tithe to Him. Tithing is for your benefit. You can find out if Jesus is really the Lord of your life when you discover how you feel about your checkbook balance.

God can help you when you bring all your tithes (one-tenth of your income) into the storehouse. This is what the God says about tithing:

Bring ye all the tithes into the storehouse, that there may be meat in mine house, and prove me now herewith, saith the Lord of hosts, if I will not open you the windows of heaven, and pour you out a blessing, that there shall not be room enough to receive it.

And I will rebuke the devourer for your sakes, and he shall not destroy the fruits of your ground; neither shall your vine cast her fruit before the time in the field, saith the Lord of hosts.

Malachi 3:10,11

Satan is the devourer, and if he is eating everything you own, it may be because you are not paying your tithes. God wants you to tithe for your benefit and for the Church's benefit, so the Gospel can be preached to every nation.

Are Your Motives Right?

If you pay your tithes out of fear, that's the wrong motive. I pay my tithes because I love my heavenly Father.

Do you feed and clothe your children because you have to, or do you take care of them because you love them? Those children were not given to you to raise and then send them out to make a living for you.

How much more should you pay your tithes to your loving heavenly Father? And how much more should you give your offerings to Him because He loves you and He gave His Son for you?

You can put "cornerstones" on your property by announcing, "Satan, I am a doer of the Word. I am a tither. There is no strife or unforgiveness in my life. You have no right to touch my property. *Satan, don't touch my stuff!*"

God said that He would rebuke the devourer for your sake. And if God rebukes him, he cannot devour the fruit of your ground, your paycheck, your business, or anything else in your life if you walk according to the Word of God.

Clause 3: Worry

Worry is not believing what the Word of God says. Worry is a sin. When you say, "I wonder if my family member is ever going to be saved...I wonder if God is ever going to answer my prayer...What is this world coming to?" you tie the hands of the Lord.

You can't receive the promises of God, because you really don't believe what *the Word* says; you are believing what *circumstances* are telling you.

The Israelites could not enter into the Promised Land because of their unbelief, according to Hebrews 3.

So we see that they were not able to enter [into His rest] because of their unwillingness to adhere to and trust and rely on God — unbelief that shut them out.

Hebrews 3:19 *The Amplified Bible*

In summary, First Peter 5:7 states, "Casting all your care upon him; for he careth for you." "All your care" means every care you have. If you will do this, Satan cannot bring the charge of worry against you.

Clause 4: Exalting One's Self

First Peter 5:6 says, "Humble yourselves therefore under the mighty hand of God, that he may exalt you in due time." "Exalt" in the Greek means that God will "put you above and on high."

You may ask, "How can I humble myself?" There is a vast difference between what religious tradition says about humility and the true meaning of it.

Some people actually become religious egotists when they think (erroneously) that they are humbling themselves.

A religious egotist will say "I will just lie down and accept this sickness, because God is going to teach me something through it." That person is ignorant of what the Word says about healing, and he will perish because of his lack of knowledge!

I asked the Lord, "What is a humble man?"

The Lord answered, "A humble man is one who will take counsel from someone else." You need to take counsel from the Lord — and you will find that counsel in His Word.

You are *not* being humble if you listen to what your body says. You are *not* being humble when you look at your bank book and say, "What are we going to do?" You are being an egotist, because you are being moved by circumstances instead of being humble and acting on God's Word.

God said you should humble yourself under His mighty hand, or under the Word of God, and *He would exalt you in due time.* "Due time" is right on time! When you need a miracle, you will be exalted in due time. Do not allow Satan to charge you with being a religious egotist and exalting yourself.

Clause 5: Gossiping

Another situation where the accuser has a legal right to put something on you is when you *gossip* about someone.

I used to gossip: "Did you hear what happened to Sister So-and-so? We are going to pray for her, but do you know what she said?" I was gossiping right in the prayer meeting!

The Bible has something to say about gossiping and being a busybody. One such scripture is found in First Timothy 5:

> Moreover, as they go about from house to house they learn to be idlers, and not only idlers but gossips and busybodies, saying what they should not say and talking of things they should not mention.
>
> I would have younger [widows] marry, bear children, guide the household, [and] not give opponents of the faith occasion for slander or reproach.
>
> For already some [widows] have turned aside after Satan.
>
> 1 Timothy 5:13-15 *The Amplified Bible*

Give occasion to whom? The accuser of the brethren!

> He who does not slander with his tongue, nor does evil to his friend, nor takes up a reproach against his neighbor...he who does these things shall not be moved.
>
> Psalm 15:3,5 *The Amplified Bible*

81

Satan, the accuser, cannot move against me, because I have purposed not to gossip anymore; I have purposed to love my fellowman; and I choose to walk in the Word. *Satan has nothing in me!*

When the Accuser Sued Me

And why do you not judge what is just, and personally decide what is right?

Then, as you go with your accuser before a magistrate, on the way make diligent effort to settle and be quit of him, lest he drag you to the judge, and the judge turn you over to the officer, and the officer put you in prison.

I tell you, you will never get out until you have paid the very last (fraction of a) cent.

Luke 12:57-59 *The Amplified Bible*

This passage is saying, in other words, "Get into forgiveness. Refuse strife. Obey the Word concerning the paying of your tithes, lest the accuser bring you up before the judge. And if he is right concerning the things he is accusing you of, you will have to pay the price for that sin."

People started asking me, "Why aren't my prayers being answered? You go around preaching that the Word works, but it isn't working for me!"

It was then that the Lord started showing me something about Satan, the accuser of the brethren. He showed me how to keep the accuser from getting anything on me! He said that I must stay in love — I must walk in love and forgiveness.

If you will just smile at those whom the devil is attempting to use to haul you into a spiritual court and say, "Brother, I love you anyway" or, "Sister, I love you anyway," no one can harm you. You can confess, "I'm a lover, and they can't hurt a lover, because Jesus is in me, and Satan has nothing in me."

How Jesus Handled the Accuser

The Pharisees and religious leaders were going to stone Jesus. But because Satan had nothing in Jesus, they could not touch Him. The Word tells us that Jesus moved through the midst of the crowd and walked away, and they could not lay a hand on Him.

You can do what Jesus did! You can say, "No weapon that is formed against me shall prosper. Any word that is exalted against me shall be pulled down."

There are many things you need to do to keep the accuser away from you. You must forgive things that happened to you many years ago. For example, you must forgive that father, mother, or anyone else who did you wrong in your past. You even have to forgive that person across town who said something to you several years ago that was unkind and caused you much grief.

A Letter of Forgiveness

I once had to write a letter to a pastor I knew. I loved him, but I became irritated with him because of some things he had said to me and some things he had said about me to other people.

I was planning to preach on unforgiveness one night. As I was praying and studying in my cabin in the woods, preparing for the meeting, I said, "God, I can't go down there and preach to all those people about unforgiveness unless You first check me out and make sure that I do not have any unforgiveness in *my* heart."

He said, "Now that you mention it, I want you to write a letter."

I said, "Yes, but, but, but... You *know* what he said about me!"

He said, "Write that letter."

I didn't do it then. I returned to the city and went to the service. It was snowing very hard that night, and right in the middle of my sermon about unforgiveness, I heard a loud noise outside: BANG!

I said, "O my God, Satan has put a spiritual lawsuit on me!"

I rushed outside and found that an elderly man had become blinded by the snowstorm, and had hit my car, smashing the rear end.

You may think, "God did that to teach you something."

No! God did not do that to me. Satan did it to me because I allowed it. While I was preparing for that meeting, God was trying to get across to me that the devil was going to put a spiritual lawsuit on me if I did not get out of unforgiveness.

It did not take me long to write that letter! The pastor answered a week later and said, "Yes, it is your fault." I got angry then and had to struggle against unforgiveness, but I continued to walk in forgiveness, and Satan had nothing in me.

This forgiveness walk — this love walk — is the best thing that ever happened to me. It was at this point that my ministry changed. I don't believe that faith will work without power behind it, and that power is love. The Bible tells us in Ephesians 5:6 that *faith works by love.*

When I decided to forgive that pastor and I mailed that letter, things started happening! There was a release in my ministry. Finances began flowing in. I choose to walk in love and forgiveness, and Satan has nothing in me!

But I say to you that every one who continues to be angry with his brother or harbors malice [enmity of heart] against him shall be liable to and unable to escape the punishment imposed by the court; and whosoever speaks contemptuously and insultingly to his brother shall be liable to and unable to escape the punishment imposed by the Sanhedrin, and whosoever says, You cursed fool! — You empty-headed idiot! shall be liable to and unable to escape the hell (Gehenna) of fire.

So if, when you are offering your gift at the altar you there remember that your brother has any [grievance] against you,

Leave your gift at the altar and go; first make peace with your brother, and then come back and present your gift.

Come to terms quickly with your accuser while you are on the way travelling with him, lest your accuser hand you over to the judge, and the judge to the guard, and you be put in prison;

Truly, I say to you, you will never be released until you have paid the last fraction of a penny.

Matthew 5:22-26 *The Amplified Bible*

The Word is telling you to first reconcile with your brother, if your brother has anything against you. Leave your tithes and offerings at the altar and go make peace with him. Then you must come to terms with your accuser while things are still going well for you, lest at any time the accuser deliver you to the judge, and God can do nothing about it because you are walking in unforgiveness and lack of love. If this happens, the accuser will slap a lawsuit on you.

Don't let this happen to you!

Stopping the Accuser

You don't have to allow Satan to push you around! Although he is standing daily before God, accusing you, he can't put a lawsuit on you if you are walking in love and obeying the Word.

Satan is a bunch of hot air! He is always trying to blow trouble your way; that is, he is trying to get you into strife, unbelief, and unforgiveness.

You can stop the accuser if you will just stick the Word down his throat. He can't blow any hot air on you if you let him have it with the Word of God. Have you ever seen the devil with a big, thick Bible stuffed in his mouth?

I saw him once when he was going around trying to stir up trouble. I attacked him with the Word and ran him off.

A man once said to me, "I am really in trouble. I am undergoing a test and a trial."

James 1:2 says, "My brethren, count it all joy when ye fall into divers temptations."

The man went on to say, "I am suffering this for Jesus."

I said, "Why don't you do what Jesus did, then?"

What did Jesus do? He quoted the Word to Satan when the enemy came and tempted Him. Jesus said, "It is written...."

I said, "Go through it like James said, and count it all joy."

The man replied, "Yeah, but I have to climb over that mountain so I will become a better Christian."

No! God doesn't do those things to you to make you a better person. You allow the accuser to bring a lawsuit against you when you do not walk according to the Word.

How To Move That Mountain

There is a better way. I do not want to *dig* mountains down. I would rather *blow them up* with my faith and let them slide into the ocean. After they disappear, I can start planting fruit where the mountains once stood.

The Bible is loaded with instructions on how to walk in the Word. You need to get in the Word and learn those instructions.

If your needs are not being met, you need to get busy and dig out the instructions. Go before the Lord and say, "Lord, I am missing it. I know it isn't You. Show me where the adversary is putting a lawsuit on me."

If we [freely] admit that we have sinned and confess our sins, He is faithful and just [true to His own nature and promises] and will forgive our sins (dismiss our lawlessness) and continuously cleanse us from all unrighteousness —everything not in conformity to His will in purpose, thought and action.

1 John 1:9 *The Amplified Bible*

When you go to the Father and ask Him to forgive you, *you are forgiven.* Even so, Satan will still come and threaten you with a lawsuit. He will say, "You have *sinned*, and you are not going to get your prayers answered."

Just quote the above scripture verse to him. It says that God has *already* forgiven you, and He *continuously* cleanses you from all unrighteousness. The devil won't dare bring that charge before heaven's court, because you are walking in the Word of God.

The only way Satan can slap a lawsuit on you is to prove that you are not conforming to the Word of God. And the only way he can prove that you are guilty is by the Word. So keep your spiritual conduits clean and walk in love. Then there is nothing you can't get from God.

Matthew 6:33 tells us:

But seek ye first the kingdom of God, and his righteousness; and all these things shall be added unto you.

We are told that the Jews are being blessed of God, and that is right. *But so am I!* I got grafted in through Jesus!

Forasmuch then as the children are partakers of flesh and blood, he also himself likewise took part of the same; that through death he might destroy him that had the power of death, that is, the devil;

And deliver them who through fear of death were all their lifetime subject to bondage.

For verily he took not on him the nature of angels; but he took on him the seed of Abraham.

Wherefore in all things it behooved him to be made like unto his brethren, that he might be a merciful and faithful high priest in things pertaining to God, to make reconciliation for the sins of the people.

Hebrews 2:14-17

Jesus is our High Priest — our Advocate, our Lawyer.

Joint-Heirs With Christ!

The Spirit itself beareth witness with our spirit, that we are the children of God:

And if children, then heirs; heirs of God, and joint-heirs with Christ; if so be that we suffer with him, that we may be also glorified together.

Romans 8:16,17

God, our Father, is the same yesterday, today, and forever. He will never increase in knowledge, because He *is* all knowledge. He will never increase in wisdom, because He *is* all wisdom.

It was God's will for you to be healed yesterday; it is His will for you to receive your healing today; and it will be His will for you to be healed tomorrow. God's will is always for you to be healed.

Someone will say, "When we get to heaven, there will be no sickness or poverty."

That's right. But you do not have to wait until you get to heaven to enjoy health and prosperity. You do not have to be ill or poor down here. The provision has been made for you: Jesus paid it all for you on the cross.

Of course, the accuser will try to put sickness and poverty on you, but you can put out his fire with the Word!

David knew that God was a covenant-keeping God. Solomon, David's son, also knew that God kept His Word. What David and Solomon got, Ed Dufresne gets. And what Ed Dufresne gets, you can get, because *God is no respecter of persons* (Acts 10:34). And you do not have to wait until you get to heaven to enjoy His promises!

When Jesus returns to this earth, the accuser is going to be tied up for a thousand years. Then he will be loosed for a short time before Jesus casts him into the lake of fire forever.

Some Final Advice

Get into the Word of God and read the instructions. Walk in love and forgiveness, and the accuser won't be able to haul you into court.

I have obeyed God by writing this book. May you be blessed by this teaching, and not allow the accuser to pin a lawsuit on you or *"steal your stuff."*

In closing, let's look at this important passage from the Instruction Book:

> My little children, I write you these things so that you may not violate God's law and sin; but if any one should sin, we have an Advocate (One Who will intercede for us) with the Father; [it is] Jesus Christ [the all] righteous — upright,

just, Who conforms to the Father's will in every purpose, thought and action.

And He — that same Jesus Himself — is the propitiation (the atoning sacrifice) for our sins, and not for ours alone, but also for [the sins of] the whole world.

And this is how we may discern [daily by experience] that we are coming to know Him — to perceive, recognize, understand and become better acquainted with Him: if we keep (bear in mind, observe, practice) His teachings (precepts, commandments).

1 John 2:1-3 The Amplified Bible

For more information about Ed Dufresne Ministries, to be placed on the mailing list or if you have a prayer request, please contact the ministry at the address listed below:

Ed Dufresne Ministries
P.O. Box 186
Temecula, CA 92593